DUKE

THE
OFFICIAL
JOHN
WAYNE
MOVIE
BOOK

FOREWORD BY
ANN-MARGRET

AFTERWORD BY
LEONARD MALTIN

John Wayne and
Ann-Margret on
the set of *The Train
Robbers* (1973).

FOREWORD

BY ANN-MARGRET, DUKE'S CO-STAR IN *THE TRAIN ROBBERS*

BY THE TIME I began my career in the 1960s, John Wayne was already a legend of the silver screen with decades of classic films behind him, from *Stagecoach* to *The Searchers*. As a newcomer to the acting business, with hopes for a long and fulfilling career, to meet and work with John was a dream. To call him a friend was, and still is, an honor.

On the set of our film *The Train Robbers*, the stories I had heard about what it was like to work with John Wayne were quickly proved true. He really was larger-than-life. Big hugs. Wide smile. Booming laugh. A charisma and presence as big as his boots. Between scenes, he was as kind as one could be. He welcomed my parents to the set as warmly as he would a pair of houseguests. That alone made him outstanding in my eyes, but John Wayne was never outdone. During the production of *The Train Robbers*, I was nominated for a Best Supporting Actress Academy Award for my role in *Carnal Knowledge* but assumed I could not attend the ceremony due to our shoot in Durango, Mexico. John, however, was not about to let me miss the milestone. In insisting that I use his private plane, not only did I attend the Oscars in Los Angeles, but I was back on set in Durango the next day!

Although I didn't come back with that coveted statuette, working with John Wayne was its own golden opportunity.

And work he did. Watching John Wayne shoot a movie later in his career, a seasoned and well-established actor, was an education in professionalism. He didn't just know his lines—he knew his characters and respected their motivations, even if they did not always square with his own. For him, it wasn't just the words; it was the why behind the words that was important. He understood what words meant to the story and how each one revealed a little something more about his character.

What I learned on the set of *The Train Robbers* influenced me for that "long and fulfilling career" I envisioned. Working with John Wayne, however briefly, marked an important turning point in my career that I consider especially influential. He was, to me and many other actors of my era, one of the greatest to ever do it. His legend lives on, in my memory, and in the memories of countless others today.

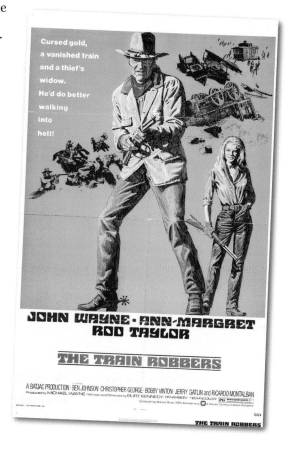

A one sheet for *The Train Robbers* (1973).

EDITORS' NOTE

AS THE EDITORS of *The Official John Wayne Collector's Edition* magazine, we are constantly reminded of the incredible feat that is Duke's body of work. In this book, as we track John Wayne's journey through 50 years of cinema by featuring every film he ever appeared in, our goal is to tell a story fit for the silver screen: that of a down-on-his-luck prop man who became an American icon.

The early sections of this book largely feature films in which Duke was an uncredited extra or, at best, an unproven newcomer. As such, our critical analysis of these films is fairly sparse—a reflection of the era in which the world had not yet met John Wayne. In the post-*Stagecoach* decades of Duke's career, our coverage expands, and we highlight many of the star's classics via in-depth Cinema Spotlight features, detailing behind-the-scenes anecdotes, critical reception and cultural impact.

As you read through these pages chronicling his career, you'll see that Duke's journey to the top of the Hollywood mountain was not without its share of setbacks. But as his character Breck Coleman prophetically stated in 1930's *The Big Trail*, the very film that first introduced the actor as "John Wayne," "No great trail was ever built without hardship."

CONTENTS

John Wayne
and Lois Moran
in *Words and
Music* (1929).

THE LEGEND BEGINS

Before he was John Wayne, Duke spent the 1920s
working his way up from uncredited extra to minor character.

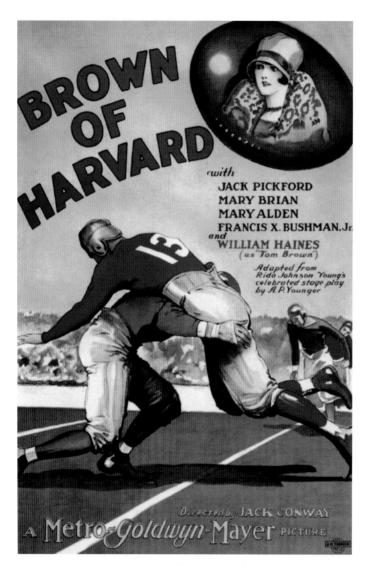

Brown of Harvard

RELEASE 1926
DIRECTOR JACK CONWAY

EVEN IN HIS first film, one thing was clear: Duke was a rookie with a ton of potential. When director Jack Conway needed to fill the field for his 1926 football flick *Brown of Harvard*, Duke's physical capabilities proved useful beyond carrying props across the lot. The film centers on a climactic clash between Harvard and Yale on the gridiron, but the realism of the game depicted was actually made possible by USC footballers. Joined by fellow Trojans rounding out both teams, Duke doubled for actor Francis X. Bushman Jr., who plays Bob McAndrew in the film, on the Yale side. While it's easy to miss, Duke's appearance in *Brown of Harvard* will forever be special for being his first.

"No doubt about the gridiron battle being the best the screen has yet held within a picture."

—*VARIETY*
May 5, 1926

★ ★ ★

Bardelys the Magnificent

RELEASE 1926
DIRECTOR KING VIDOR

IN THE COURT OF King Louis VIII, suave courtier Marquis Christian de Bardelys (John Gilbert) develops a reputation as a ladies' man. Duke puts his imposing presence to use as a guard in this uncredited role.

The Great K&A Train Robbery

RELEASE 1926
DIRECTOR LEWIS SEILER

HIRED TO STOP the recurring train robberies on the local railroad, the fearless Tom Gordon (Tom Mix) goes undercover as a highwayman. After initially only being hired as a prop worker, Duke found himself appearing as an uncredited extra in the film.

The Draw-Back

RELEASE 1927
DIRECTOR NORMAN TAUROG

A MEEK YOUNG MAN becomes the favorite target of bullies once he arrives at college, prompting his wife to sign him up for the football team. Duke can be seen putting his pigskin past to use once again as an extra on the gridiron in this 26-minute short.

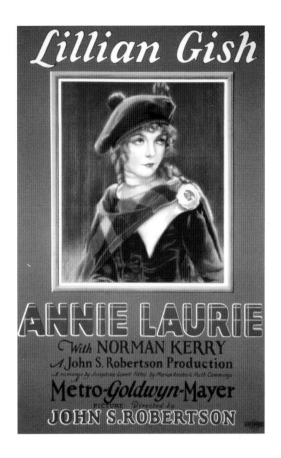

Annie Laurie

RELEASE 1927
DIRECTOR JOHN S. ROBERTSON

IN THE MIDDLE OF the ongoing battle between the Scottish clans Campbell and MacDonald, a young girl named Annie Laurie (Lillian Gish) finds herself in a romance with a member of the opposing side. Duke plays an extra in a crowd scene.

The Drop Kick

RELEASE 1927
DIRECTOR MILLARD WEBB

THIS SILENT SPORTS drama sees Richard Barthelmess as Jack Hamill, a college football player blamed for a man's death. The film provided Duke another uncredited role as a football player.

Seeing Stars

RELEASE 1927
DIRECTOR STEPHEN ROBERTS

IN THIS SHORT comedy, a young Duke stands tall in his small role—which was officially listed as "Tall Boy." The 20-minute film sees two men stargazing across America.

Seeing Stars features Pal the Dog, a collie who starred in many shorts in the 1920s.

Mother Machree

RELEASE 1928
DIRECTOR JOHN FORD

AFTER HERDING GEESE on the set of this film as part of his job as a stage hand, Duke caught the attention of John Ford and landed a role as an extra. The rest, of course, is history.

Four Sons

RELEASE 1928
DIRECTOR JOHN FORD

IN HIS SECOND film helmed by his soon-to-be-mentor, Duke plays an officer in the background of a scene. The film tells the story of three Bavarian brothers who go to war for Germany while the fourth fights on the American side.

"A profoundly moving picture of family life in Germany during the war."

—VARIETY
February 15, 1928

★ ★ ★

WILLIAM FOX
PRESENTS

FOUR SONS

BIG
AS THE HEART
of HUMANITY

JOHN FORD
PRODUCTION

Like Duke, director Norman Taurog worked as a propman before making it big.

A Home-Made Man

RELEASE **1928**
DIRECTOR **NORMAN TAUROG**

IN THIS SHORT about a soda jerk fumbling his way through a new job at a physical fitness club for men, Duke can be seen sitting on a stool at the club's lunch counter.

Hangman's House

RELEASE **1928**
DIRECTOR **JOHN FORD**

EXILED IRISH PATRIOT "Citizen" Hogan (Victor McLaglen) risks it all to return to his homeland and settle a family matter. John Ford again gave his propman Duke some on-camera work as a steeplechase spectator in one scene.

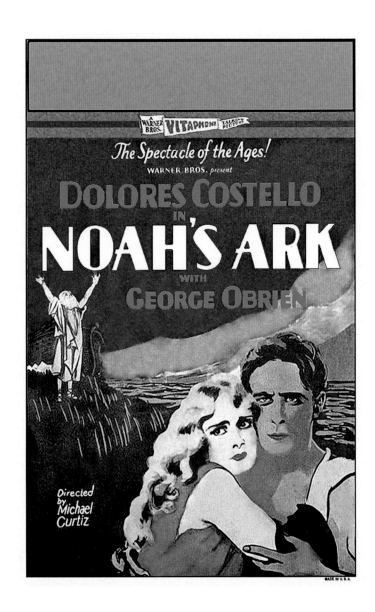

Noah's Ark

RELEASE 1928
DIRECTOR MICHAEL CURTIZ

WELL BEFORE HE made the instant classic *Casablanca* (1942), director Michael Curtiz worked with an eventual icon of American cinema, John Wayne. For his telling of the Biblical story of Noah and the Great Flood that drew parallels to the events of World War I, Curtiz turned his lens toward Duke and his pal Ward Bond, who worked as extras in one of the film's flood scenes. Curtiz and John Wayne would go on to work together on two more occasions, in 1953 for *Trouble Along the Way* and in 1961 for *The Comancheros*, Curtiz's final film.

Strong Boy

RELEASE 1929
DIRECTOR JOHN FORD

PULLING DOUBLE DUTY for his eventual mentor, Duke worked as a propman behind the scenes and also appeared as an extra in this silent comedy from John Ford. Now considered a lost film, a trailer for this picture was discovered in the New Zealand Film Archive in 2010.

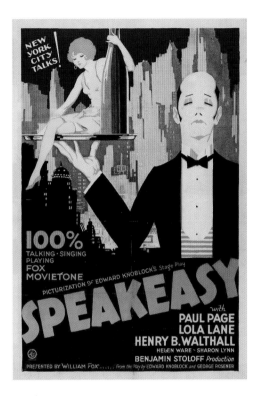

Speakeasy

RELEASE 1929
DIRECTOR BENJAMIN STOLOFF

IN PURSUIT OF a story on boxer Paul Martin (Paul Page) newspaper reporter Alice Woods (Lola Lane) follows the fighter to the speakeasy he frequents. Duke worked as an uncredited extra for the film and appeared in the background of one scene.

The Black Watch

RELEASE 1929
DIRECTOR JOHN FORD

The Black Watch is notable for being the first "talkie" directed by John Ford.

CAPTAIN DONALD KING (Victor McLaglen) goes to India at the start of World War I on a secret mission to rescue captured British soldiers. Duke has an uncredited role as one of the many 42nd Highlanders seen in the film.

Words and Music

RELEASE 1929
DIRECTOR JAMES TINLING

IN HIS FIRST significant role, John Wayne (credited as Duke Morrison) plays Phil Donahue, a fraternity member hoping to convince the talented Mary Brown (Lois Moran) to lead the musical numbers in his school's annual revue.

Lois Moran and John Wayne in *Words and Music* (1929).

"He doesn't mean the audience. What do the actors do, Mister?"

—JOHN WAYNE
AS MIDSHIPMAN BILL

★ ★ ★

Salute

RELEASE 1929
DIRECTOR JOHN FORD

AFTER BEING A nameless, voiceless, blink-and-you'll-miss-him figure in several films, Duke would finally get the opportunity to work as an actual character with a memorable line of dialogue. Only a few years removed from the disappointment of not being admitted to the U.S. Naval Academy, Duke was given the chance to don the blue uniform to play Midshipman Bill in this John Ford sports drama about the famed football rivalry between Army and Navy. The film also features Duke's former USC pal Ward Bond in a similar role as Midshipman Harold.

George O'Brien and John Wayne in *Salute* (1929).

John Ford (with megaphone) and John Wayne (far right) on the set of *Men Without Women* (1930).

John Wayne is rumored to have been an extra in the film *The Lone Star Ranger* (1930).

The Forward Pass

RELEASE **1929**
DIRECTOR **EDWARD F. CLINE**

DUKE RETURNS TO his recurring role of an uncredited football player for this sports drama about Marty Reid (Douglas Fairbanks Jr.), a star quarterback at Sanford College facing harsh conflicts off the field.

Men Without Women

RELEASE **1930**
DIRECTOR **JOHN FORD**

CHIEF TORPEDOMAN BURKE (Kenneth MacKenna) and his crew struggle to stay alive long enough for rescuers to reach them after their submarine, the U.S. S13, sinks. Duke appears as a radioman on land.

Born Reckless

RELEASE **1930**
DIRECTOR **JOHN FORD**

DUKE APPEARS AS an extra in this crime drama about newspaper reporter Bill O'Brien's (Lee Tracy) successful campaign to send criminal Louis Beretti (Edmund Lowe) and his cronies to fight in the war as punishment for their involvement in an armed robbery.

Rough Romance

RELEASE **1930**
DIRECTOR **A.F. ERICKSON**

A YOUNG DUKE puts his rugged physicality to good use as an uncredited lumberjack in this film about a Canadian lumber worker who witnesses a murder and finds himself being stalked by the fur thieves guilty of the crime.

Cheer Up and Smile

RELEASE **1930**
DIRECTOR **SIDNEY LANFIELD**

A RADIO SINGER is knocked unconscious during a robbery, which leads a shrill student to spontaneously fill in. Oddly enough, the young man becomes an overnight sensation. Duke appears as a background character named Roy.

John Wayne (front row, third from right) on the set of *Cheer Up and Smile* (1930).

From left: Harry Cording, George O'Brien, John Wayne and Antonio Moreno in *Rough Romance* (1930).

John Wayne on the set of *The Big Trail* (1930).

A STAR IS BORN

Once he was dubbed John Wayne, Duke spent the 1930s climbing the ranks as a tireless leading man.

The Big Trail

RELEASE 1930
DIRECTOR RAOUL WALSH

BEFORE HE WAS capturing the imaginations of moviegoers across the country, John Wayne's time in Hollywood was devoted more to blue-collar work than silver screen stardom. The eventual innovator of the Western genre first dipped his toes into the industry working as a propman and occasional extra for director John Ford in the 1920s. But in 1930, the 23-year-old's life would change overnight when he went from nameless face in the background straight to the leading role of an epic production.

Inspired by a *Saturday Evening Post* serial by Hal G. Evarts called "The Shaggy Legion," director Raoul Walsh approached Fox Film Corporation executives with the idea for the film that would become *The Big Trail* (1930). Determined to remain faithful to Evarts's story about a true frontiersman who leads a wagon of hundreds of pioneers through countless hardships, Walsh felt the authenticity needed for the lead of Breck Coleman could only be achieved by a Hollywood newcomer. "I don't want an actor," the director told the studio, according to Scott Eyman's biography *John Wayne: The Life and Legend*. "I want someone to get out there and act natural—be himself. I'll make an actor out of him if need be."

On a visit to the set of John Ford's film *Born Reckless* in 1930, Walsh would find just the fresh face he was looking for.

According to documentarian (and friend of Walsh) Richard Schickel, the bold director noticed Duke's impressive physical presence as the young man was lugging furniture around.

"Walsh says he saw Wayne carrying a chair or something in the props department," Schickel told *True West* magazine in 2008. "And, as he tells the story, he went over to [Duke] and chatted with him and asked if he wanted to be in a picture.

And they did a test—I don't think it was a talking test—it was a kind of in-costume, silent test. And they put him in a nice pair of buckskins, which he wore in the picture, and asked, 'How'd you like to be an actor?' And he said, 'I'd like to do that.'"

Before the ambitious propman could truly become an actor, though, he needed a name becoming of a star. As Duke is quoted as saying in *John Wayne: The Life and Legend*, "Duke Morrison would sound too much like a stuntman or something, and Marion Morrison would have probably got me in more fights than I'd normally get in." The name "Wayne" would come first, thanks to studio head Winfield Sheehan, who was a fan of Revolutionary War general Mad Anthony Wayne, while "John" merely felt like a natural fit for the surname. "I didn't have any say in it, but I think it's a great name," the legend later reflected in a 1971 interview. "It's short and strong and to the point."

Newly christened with a powerful moniker, John Wayne was ready to lead the Western genre into new territory when *The Big Trail* hit theaters on November 1, 1930. As Breck Coleman, Duke

4

unknowingly gave a glimpse into the future of his career, exhibiting many of the motivations and traits that would define countless characters he would later play. Coleman is a fearless fur trapper looking to track down Red Flack (Tyrone Power Sr.) and Lopez (Charles Stevens), the men who murdered his friend and fellow trapper. Once he discovers that the two are heading west along the Oregon Trail, Coleman accepts a request to scout a large caravan of settlers as they attempt to take the same dangerous route, officially establishing John Wayne as the heroic he-man the world would see him as for decades to come.

Raoul Walsh was not only looking to make a new star

1. John Wayne in *The Big Trail* (1930). **2.** Ward Bond and Duke on the set of the film. **3.** Promotional artwork for *The Big Trail*. **4.** Duke and Marguerite Churchill in *The Big Trail*.

"No great trail was ever built without hardship."

—JOHN WAYNE AS BRECK COLEMAN

★ ★ ★

6

tableau editing combine to make a statement quite different from that of the typical Hollywood film," wrote critic Fred Camper in a 1988 retrospective review in the *Chicago Reader*. "Walsh has given us a rare vision of nature, one that is not man-centered; his film is permeated with a powerful, mysterious sense of an always-looming, weighty abstracted empty space."

While *The Big Trail* came up short at the box office and was ultimately considered a financial disappointment, in part due to the circumstances of the Great Depression, the Western undeniably succeeded in taking the genre to exciting new territory. Plus, John Wayne's debut starring role was anything but a failure. Critic Mordaunt Hall wrote in his review in *The New York Times*, "Mr. Wayne acquits himself with no little distinction. His performance is pleasingly natural." John Wayne had delivered exactly the type of performance Raoul Walsh was looking for, and his career as a charismatic leading man audiences could easily get behind was just beginning.

with *The Big Trail*, he was also aiming to launch the Western genre as a whole into a new stratum of artistry. During production, the director demanded extensive outdoor shoots featuring 20,000 extras, almost 200 covered wagons and thousands of cattle and horses. Adding to the complexity of the undertaking was the use of 70mm cameras, allowing cinematographer Arthur Edeson to capture scenes of breathtaking scope at the cost of constant care and upkeep of the lenses—which was no easy task considering the film shot in harsh environments such as Yuma, Arizona, and Jackson Hole, Wyoming. "It became a hard and fast rule that the cameras must be cleaned thoroughly every night, not only with brushes, but with compressed air streams," wrote Edeson in the September 1930 issue of *American Cinematographer*. Despite the daunting challenges confronting Walsh and his team, the movie's epic scope and breathtaking spectacle have continued to awe audiences for generations. "The oddly meditative quality of Walsh's long takes, the curious lack of a dominant narrative tension controlling the film's space and the oddly disjunct tableau-to-

7

5. John Wayne and an uncredited Crow Tribe member in *The Big Trail*. **6.** A premiere program for the film. **7.** Tully Marshall (background left), El Brendel, John Wayne and Ward Bond (background right).

Girls Demand Excitement

RELEASE **1931**
DIRECTOR **SEYMOUR FELIX**

THIS ROMANTIC COMEDY sees Duke as Peter Brooks, a gruff college student who has no interest in allowing women to interfere with his studies—that is until he meets charming socialite Joan (Virginia Cherrill).

Three Girls Lost

RELEASE **1931**
DIRECTOR **SIDNEY LANFIELD**

DUKE'S GORDON WALES flirts with his neighbor Marcia (Joan Marsh) while she's locked out of her apartment. When Marcia is found murdered soon after, Wales is a prime suspect.

Arizona

RELEASE **1931**
DIRECTOR **GEORGE B. SEITZ**

DUKE STARS AS Lt. Bob Denton, a West Point football star who can't commit to his girlfriend Evelyn (Laura La Plante), which prompts her to marry his mentor Col. Bonham (Forrest Stanley) as an act of revenge. In the aftermath of losing his lady, Bob changes his ways and falls hard for Bonita (June Clyde), Evelyn's sister.

The Deceiver

RELEASE **1931**
DIRECTOR **LOUIS KING**

BEFORE HE COULD stand tall as the hero in all of his films, Duke had to be patient—and in this case, remain very still. In this 1931 film, an actor is found dead in his dressing room with a knife sticking out of his back, prompting a classic whodunit. Duke's character is off the hook from the start though, as is his only contribution to the film is serving as a stand-in for the corpse at the center of the mystery.

"Some good old murder mystery entertainment."

—*THE FILM DAILY*
November 29, 1931

★ ★ ★

The Deceiver director Louis King was initially slated to direct The Range Feud.

The Range Feud

RELEASE **1931**
DIRECTOR **D. ROSS LEDERMAN**

TANGLED UP IN a land battle thanks to his romantic involvement with the daughter of a rancher, Duke's Clint Turner finds himself accused of murder.

Maker of Men

RELEASE **1931**
DIRECTOR **EDWARD SEDGWICK**

THIS SPORTS DRAMA sees Duke returning to his roots as a gridiron star named Dusty Rhodes, the most popular and skilled player on the team, who has no patience for his struggling teammate Bob (Richard Cromwell).

Texas Cyclone

RELEASE **1932**
DIRECTOR **D. ROSS LEDERMAN**

WHEN A COWBOY called Texas Grant (Tim McCoy) rides into town, everyone believes him to be the presumed-dead rancher Jim Rawlings. Grant leans into the confusion and associates himself with John Wayne's ranch hand Steve.

John Wayne, Lloyd Whitlock and Dorothy Gulliver in *The Shadow of the Eagle* (1932).

The Shadow of the Eagle

RELEASE **1932**
DIRECTOR **FORD BEEBE**

ON THE HUNT for a mysterious criminal called "The Eagle" who makes threats via skywriting, John Wayne's heroic pilot Craig McCoy takes flight in an attempt to crack the case. After the disappearance of Colonel Nathan Gregory (Edward Hearn), a veteran pilot who runs a struggling carnival, many believe The Eagle is Gregory himself. This film serial is a major milestone in Duke's career as it marked the first time he worked with stuntman Yakima Canutt, his partner in creating the style of cinematic fist-fighting known as the "pass system" as well as the inspiration for much of the John Wayne persona.

Two-Fisted Law

RELEASE 1932
DIRECTOR D. ROSS LEDERMAN

WHEN BOB RUSSELL (Wheeler Oakman) collects a debt from Tim Clark (Tim McCoy) by rustling his cattle and stealing his ranch, John Wayne's Duke says of the matter, "All I can wish for Russell is a rough horse, a cactus saddle and a long journey."

Lady and Gent

RELEASE 1932
DIRECTOR STEPHEN ROBERTS

JOHN WAYNE PUTS his dukes up as Buzz Kinney, a young boxer fresh out of college who manages to knock out Stag Bailey (George Bancroft), a veteran of the sport.

The Hurricane Express

RELEASE 1932
DIRECTORS J.P. MCGOWAN, ARMAND SCHAEFER

AFTER A TRAINWRECK kills his father, Duke's Larry Baker looks for the man responsible for causing that and several other train "accidents."

John Wayne in
Ride Him, Cowboy (1932).

The horse in *Ride Him, Cowboy* goes by his real name in the film: Duke.

John Wayne and Mae Madison in *The Big Stampede* (1932).

Ride Him, Cowboy

RELEASE 1932
DIRECTOR FRED ALLEN

EVEN IN HIS earliest films, John Wayne was delivering the justice-seeking spirit his characters would later be known for. In this 1932 film, Duke plays John Drury, the only man in town who seems to have any sense. When a horse is blamed for the death of a local man, Drury tells the irrational locals. "Where I come from, we don't shoot horses when they get ornery; we tame 'em." He rides the allegedly aggressive steed, and his instincts about the animal's innocence are soon proven correct. As it turns out, the horse was framed—the man was murdered by a notorious outlaw.

The Big Stampede

RELEASE 1932
DIRECTOR TENNY WRIGHT

SENT TO STOP cattle rustler Sam Crew (Noah Beery) and his gang, John Wayne's Deputy Sheriff John Steele recruits a bandit called Sonora Joe (Luis Alberni) to even the odds. Duke would return to the "unlikely allies teaming up for the greater good" premise a few more times later in his career, but this film remains a shining example of the icon playing a man who achieves justice through his quick wits and fists.

Haunted Gold

RELEASE 1932
DIRECTOR MACK V. WRIGHT

THIS REMAKE OF the 1928 Ken Maynard film *The Phantom City* stars Duke as John Mason, a man on the hunt for a hidden fortune in an abandoned mine. Aside from dealing with a rival gang eyeing the riches, Mason and his partner Janet Carter (Sheila Terry) also have to contend with a mysterious spirit. While merely a means for Duke to further hone his craft at the time, this amusing, action-packed oater has come to be beloved by some Western historians over the years. In his book *The Best (and Worst) of the West!*, Boyd Magers called the film "One of the most entertaining B-westerns ever made."

Jim Corey, John Wayne and Blackjack Ward in *Haunted Gold* (1932).

That's My Boy

RELEASE 1932
DIRECTOR ROY WILLIAM NEILL

THIS UNCREDITED ROLE sees John Wayne back on the football field as Taylor, a member of the Harvard team battling Bedford University.

The Telegraph Trail

RELEASE 1933
DIRECTOR TENNY WRIGHT

DUKE'S CAVALRY SCOUT John Trent pieces together evidence that reveals the recent Native American uprisings preventing the completion of new telegraph lines were a scheme devised by businessman Gus Lynch (Albert J. Smith).

The Three Musketeers

RELEASE 1933
DIRECTORS COLBERT CLARK, ARMAND SCHAEFER

IN THIS SERIAL, Duke plays aviator Tom Wayne, who, while flying over the African desert, spots and rescues a trio of Legionnaires called "The Three Musketeers" from attacking bandits.

Central Airport

RELEASE 1933
DIRECTORS WILLIAM A. WELLMAN,
ALFRED E. GREEN

THIS DISASTER FILM features a rare instance of John Wayne meeting his demise as the star plays an unnamed co-pilot who courageously goes down with a plane.

Somewhere in Sonora

RELEASE 1933
DIRECTOR MACK V. WRIGHT

DUKE THE HORSE shares the screen with John Wayne again in this B-Western about a man who tries to foil a mine-robbing plot by joining up with the criminals.

The Life of Jimmy Dolan

RELEASE 1933
DIRECTOR ARCHIE MAYO

AFTER ACCIDENTALLY KILLING a reporter in a drunken rage, boxer Jimmy Dolan (Douglas Fairbanks Jr.) takes on a false identity and fights the likes of Duke's Smith, a young man hoping to earn the prize money to take care of his wife and new baby.

John Wayne and Evalyn Knapp in *His Private Secretary* (1933).

His Private Secretary

RELEASE 1933
DIRECTOR PHIL WHITMAN

AS THE PLAYBOY Dick Wallace, Duke displays his suave side before settling down and eloping with Marion (Evalyn Knapp), who happens to take a job as a secretary at the senior Wallace's company. Since his father believes the woman to be a gold digger, Dick knows he must keep the marriage a secret.

Baby Face

RELEASE 1933
DIRECTOR ALFRED E. GREEN

JOHN WAYNE PLAYS a small role as Jimmy McCoy Jr., an office worker who falls under the spell of Lily Powers's (Barbara Stanwyck) irresistible charms.

John Wayne
in *Riders of
Destiny* (1933).

The Man from Monterey is a remake of the 1928 film The Canyon of Adventure.

The Man from Monterey

RELEASE 1933
DIRECTOR MACK V. WRIGHT

THIS FILM FEATURES John Wayne as Cavalry captain John Holmes, whose time in Old California turns turbulent when he faces off with greedy land grabbers trying to steal property from an innocent family. *Film Daily* wrote that the B-Western "packs plenty of thrills and fast action."

Riders of Destiny

RELEASE 1933
DIRECTOR ROBERT N. BRADBURY

AS SINGIN' SANDY SAUNDERS, Duke ventured into the unknown territory of playing a crooning cowboy, despite his inability to carry a tune. The singing scenes were achieved by John Wayne pseudo-strumming a guitar and lip-syncing while director Robert N. Bradbury's son Bill, a skilled vocalist, belted out the songs from off camera. During a 1971 appearance on *The Glen Campbell Goodtime Hour*, Duke joked that he still had nightmares about the role.

College Coach

RELEASE 1933
DIRECTOR WILLIAM A. WELLMAN

DUKE PLAYS A STUDENT in this sports drama about the ruthless Coach Gore (Pat O'Brien), a man obsessed with taking Calvert College's football team to the top.

Sagebrush Trail

RELEASE 1933
DIRECTOR ARMAND SCHAEFER

AFTER ESCAPING PRISON, John Wayne's John Brant heads west and joins up with a gang of outlaws. Soon after, Brant discovers that one of the men in the gang, who goes by the alias Jones (Lane Chandler) is the one who actually committed the murder that got Brant locked up.

John Wayne, Art Mix and Yakima Canutt in *Sagebrush Trail* (1933).

John Wayne and
Barbara Sheldon in *The
Lucky Texan* (1934).

The Lucky Texan shot on location in the Antelope Valley region of California.

The Lucky Texan

RELEASE **1934**
DIRECTOR **ROBERT N. BRADBURY**

DUKE AND GEORGE "GABBY" HAYES, as Jerry Mason and Jake Benson, respectively, show off their silver screen chemistry as mining partners who realize gold doesn't make life easier.

West of the Divide

RELEASE **1934**
DIRECTOR **ROBERT N. BRADBURY**

AFTER HIS FATHER is murdered, John Wayne's Ted Hayden encounters a dying outlaw named Gatt Ganns and decides to impersonate him to join a gang led by Gentry (Lloyd Whitlock), his father's murderer.

Blue Steel

RELEASE **1934**
DIRECTOR **ROBERT N. BRADBURY**

AS JOHN CARRUTHERS, John Wayne steps into the well-suited role of a U.S. Marshal who helps a town fend off a group of outlaws looking to snatch up gold that rightfully belongs to a local settlement.

John Wayne in *The Man from Utah* (1934).

The Man from Utah

RELEASE **1934**
DIRECTOR **ROBERT N. BRADBURY**

SENT TO INVESTIGATE a rodeo to find out who is behind the murders of prize-winning riders, John Wayne's John Weston becomes a target himself when the bad guys plant a poisoned needle under his saddle.

Randy Rides Alone

RELEASE 1934
DIRECTOR HARRY L. FRASER

AS TRAVELING COWBOY Randy Bowers, John Wayne got the chance to prove himself to Western-loving moviegoers just as his character worked to prove himself to finger-pointing onlookers in the film. When Bowers ventures into a rest station to take a much-needed break from his travels, he quickly realizes he's in a major "wrong place at the wrong time" scenario when he finds a pile of corpses and an empty safe. Soon, an angry crowd arrives and mistakes Bowers for a member of a murderous gang. Sally Rogers (Alberta Vaughn), however, knows the wanderer is innocent and breaks him out of jail. Determined to clear his name once and for all, Bowers decides to track down the missing money. Ironically, as he gets as far away from the sheriff as he can, Bowers ends up encountering the gang responsible for the murders and the robbery. After being recruited by leader Marvin Black (George "Gabby" Hayes), Bowers bonds with Spike (Yakima Canutt) by shooting at a wanted poster in a game of one-upmanship in a scene that remains a standout given the friendship burgeoning between Duke and his frequent stuntman and fight scene collaborator at the time.

Directed by Harry L. Fraser, who would also helm the star's 1934 Western *'Neath the Arizona Skies*, *Randy Rides Alone* gives John Wayne fans another entertaining hour of everything Duke excelled at early in his film career. In his 1976 book *John Wayne and the Movies*, Allen Eyles noted how Duke's now iconic persona was beginning to take shape: "Wayne's walk in this film has a lazy air of confidence, and he is seen twirling his six-shooter with professional ease...." Randy may have been riding alone, but John Wayne was gaining quite a following.

Artie Ortego, Earl Dwire, John Wayne and Yakima Canutt in *Randy Rides Alone* (1934).

The Star Packer

RELEASE **1934**
DIRECTOR **ROBERT N. BRADBURY**

WITH HIS COMPANION Yak (Yakima Canutt) by his side, Duke's John Travers becomes de facto sheriff and takes on an enigmatic outlaw and his gang.

The Trail Beyond

RELEASE **1934**
DIRECTOR **ROBERT N. BRADBURY**

SENT TO FIND a missing miner and his daughter, John Wayne's Rod Drew and his partner Wabi (Noah Beery Jr.) find themselves in a cat-and-mouse game with gold-seeking crooks.

The Lawless Frontier

RELEASE **1934**
DIRECTOR **ROBERT N. BRADBURY**

FOLLOWING THE MURDER of his parents, John Wayne's John Tobin sets out to find the man responsible, Pandro Zanti (Earl Dwire), leading to a thrilling chase that sees the cowboy pursuing the bandit through the desert.

This film was delayed three weeks to avoid overlap with the release of *The Lawless Frontier* (1934).

'Neath the Arizona Skies

RELEASE **1934**
DIRECTOR **HARRY L. FRASER**

AFTER BEING KNOCKED unconscious following a fall from his horse and having his clothes stolen by a fleeing robber, John Wayne's Chris Morrell wakes to the comforting care of a woman named Clara (Sheila Terry). But when Morrell later meets Clara's brother Jim (Jay Wilsey), he recognizes him as the robber, providing a satisfying early twist that lets the audience know this romance won't come without complications. Still, determined to return the favor, Morrell tries to help Clara find her missing father so she can cash in on a promised oil lease—but the two soon encounter a couple of outlaws who would gladly steal the girl's rightful riches.

Texas Terror

RELEASE **1935**
DIRECTOR **ROBERT N. BRADBURY**

AFTER BELIEVING HE killed his best friend by accident in a wild shootout with robbers, John Wayne's Sheriff John Higgins goes into exile before discovering the truth and finding the real culprits.

Sheila Terry, John Wayne and Jack Rockwell in *'Neath the Arizona Skies* (1934).

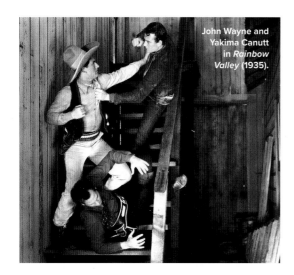

John Wayne and Yakima Canutt in *Rainbow Valley* (1935).

Rainbow Valley

RELEASE 1935
DIRECTOR ROBERT N. BRADBURY

DYNAMITE AND SUBTERFUGE color this Western that sees John Wayne as John Martin, a clever cowboy who aims to capture gunman Galt (Jay Wilsey) and his gang by seemingly giving them what they want.

The Desert Trail

RELEASE 1935
DIRECTOR LEWIS D. COLLINS

TWO RODEO RIDERS, John Wayne's John Scott and Kansas Charlie (Eddy Chandler) are accused of armed robbery. Desperate to prove their innocence, they head to Poker City to find the real culprits.

The Dawn Rider

RELEASE 1935
DIRECTOR ROBERT N. BRADBURY

AFTER BEARING WITNESS to his father's death during a robbery, John Wayne's justice-seeking John Mason vows to track down the men responsible.

Paradise Canyon

RELEASE 1935
DIRECTOR CARL PIERSON

AN UNDERCOVER AGENT, John Wayne's John Wyatt (posing as John Rogers) heads to the Mexican border to round up a group of counterfeiters causing trouble.

In 2008, *Paradise Canyon* was colorized and re-released as *Guns Along the Trail.*

Westward Ho

RELEASE 1935
DIRECTOR ROBERT N. BRADBURY

LEADING HIS GROUP of crooning cowboy vigilantes, John Wayne's John Wyatt head West to find the gang responsible for the murder of Wyatt's parents several years prior. Duke's vocals were dubbed by Jack Kirk, one of the uncredited cowboys.

John Wayne in *The Dawn Rider* (1935).

Harry Harvey,
Frank Rice and
John Wayne in *The
Oregon Trail* (1936).

The New Frontier

RELEASE **1935**
DIRECTOR **CARL PIERSON**

WHEN FREE LAND opens up in late 1800s Oklahoma, pioneers settle new towns. After self-appointed leader Ace Holmes (Warner Richmond) turns tyrannical, Duke's John Dawson teams up with outlaws to stop him.

Lawless Range

RELEASE **1935**
DIRECTOR **ROBERT N. BRADBURY**

RETURNING TO THE role of a crooning cowboy, John Wayne plays John Middleton, a rodeo star known to break into song. Jack Kirk, who dubbed Duke's singing in *Westward Ho* (1935) handled the vocals again.

The Oregon Trail

RELEASE **1936**
DIRECTOR **SCOTT PEMBROKE**

With no prints remaining, *The Oregon Trail* is considered a lost film.

DUKE'S CAPTAIN DELMONT takes a leave from the Army to lead a wagon to California in search of his father.

John Wayne in *The Lawless Nineties* (1936).

The Lawless Nineties

RELEASE **1936**
DIRECTOR **JOSEPH KANE**

AFTER HEADING TO Wyoming to oversee a vote to join the Union, John Wayne's federal agent John Tipton encounters far more trouble than he anticipated as a group of dastardly locals begins terrorizing the town with dynamite and unprovoked attacks.

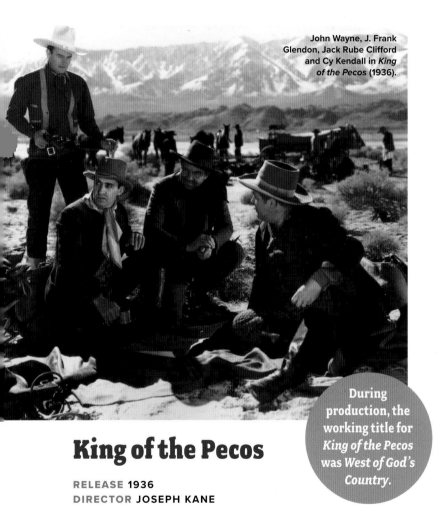

John Wayne, J. Frank Glendon, Jack Rube Clifford and Cy Kendall in *King of the Pecos* (1936).

King of the Pecos

RELEASE 1936
DIRECTOR JOSEPH KANE

TEN YEARS AFTER his parents are killed by cattle baron Alexander Stiles (Cy Kendall), John Wayne's lawyer John Clayborn tries to take the murderer down via legal action before resorting to violence.

During production, the working title for *King of the Pecos* was *West of God's Country*.

The Lonely Trail

RELEASE 1936
DIRECTOR JOSEPH KANE

DUKE'S CIVIL WAR veteran Captain John Ashley, despite being a proud Northerner, is hired by the Governor of Texas (Sam Flint) to drive out a group of carpetbaggers.

Winds of the Wasteland

RELEASE 1936
DIRECTOR MACK V. WRIGHT

OUT OF WORK following the arrival of the telegraph, Duke's Pony Express rider John Blair competes against stageline owner Cal Drake (Douglas Cosgrove) for a mail contract.

Sea Spoilers

RELEASE 1936
DIRECTOR FRANK R. STRAYER

THIS FILM SEES John Wayne as Coast Guard Commander Bob Randall, a man on a mission to rescue his kidnapped girlfriend from seal poachers. The *Motion Picture Herald* praised the film's pacing, writing, "There is much action, a substantial measure of menace and the outcome is well-cloaked until late in the film."

John Wayne and
William Bakewell in
Sea Spoilers (1936).

From left: Art Mix, unidentified, Ed Cassidy, John Wayne, Jon Hall (as Charles Locher) and Lane Chandler in *Winds of the Wasteland* (1936).

John Wayne in
Conflict (1936).

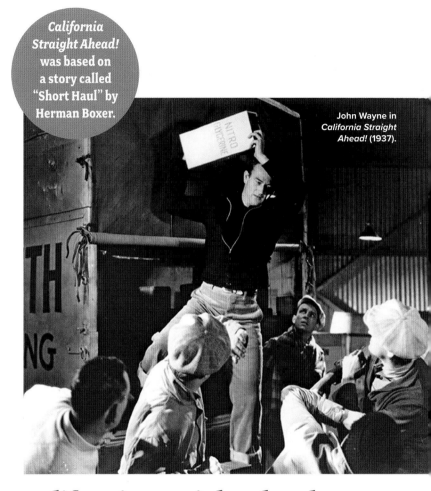

California Straight Ahead! was based on a story called "Short Haul" by Herman Boxer.

John Wayne in *California Straight Ahead!* (1937).

"Its fight scenes, in and out of the ring, are grandly directed."

—*THE NEW YORK TIMES*
January 18, 1937

★ ★ ★

Conflict

RELEASE 1936
DIRECTOR DAVID HOWARD

IN THIS ADAPTATION of the Jack London short story "The Abysmal Brute," John Wayne puts his dukes up as Pat Glendon, a logger-turned-boxer battling the idea of throwing a match against a prizefighter. *Variety* praised the early look at the star's heroic qualities and convincing fisticuffs, writing in its review, "Wayne's performance is best when he saves a kid from drowning and when he's slugging."

California Straight Ahead!

RELEASE 1937
DIRECTOR ARTHUR LUBIN

THIS FAST AND FURIOUS film features Duke as Biff Smith, a trucker who pits his fleet against a freight train in a heated race to deliver aviation parts to the Golden State.

Don Barclay and
John Wayne in *I Cover
the War!* (1937).

> *"Wayne is entirely at home in his performance, the smoothest he has ever offered..."*

—*THE HOLLYWOOD REPORTER*
July 1937

★ ★ ★

I Cover the War!

RELEASE 1937
DIRECTOR **ARTHUR LUBIN**

THOUGH HE WOULD later be known for playing heroes on the frontlines, this Universal release sees John Wayne on the other side of the action as a newsreel cameraman who travels to North Africa to document an Arab uprising.

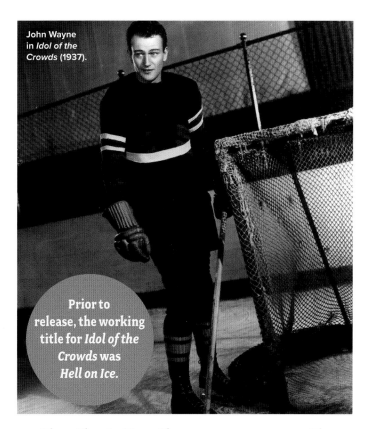

John Wayne in *Idol of the Crowds* (1937).

Prior to release, the working title for *Idol of the Crowds* was *Hell on Ice*.

Idol of the Crowds

RELEASE 1937
DIRECTOR **ARTHUR LUBIN**

JOHN WAYNE STARS as Johnny Hanson, a chicken farmer who finds fame and fortune as a professional hockey player. As part of the deal with Universal, each of the Lubin-helmed films from 1937 had extremely tight production times—meaning Duke had to push through the painful process of swiftly learning to ice skate in order to stay on schedule.

John Wayne in *Adventure's End* (1937)

Adventure's End

RELEASE 1937
DIRECTOR ARTHUR LUBIN

AS PACIFIC PEARL DIVER Duke Slade in this final entry in the rapidly produced Universal series, the actor earned praise from *Hollywood Reporter*, which wrote, "John Wayne is a likely hero...His action scenes are first-rate."

Born to the West

RELEASE 1937
DIRECTOR CHARLES BARTON

THIS WESTERNS SEES Duke as Dare Rudd, a cowhand who decides to take a job in order to have a better chance at winning the heart of the alluring Judy Worstall (Marsha Hunt).

Syd Saylor and John Wayne in *Born to the West* (1937).

Born to the West **was rereleased in 1950 as** *Hell Town.*

John Wayne in *Pals of the Saddle* (1938).

Pals of the Saddle

RELEASE 1938
DIRECTOR GEORGE SHERMAN

IN HIS FIRST outing as one of the Three Mesquiteers, John Wayne impressed critics, with *Variety* claiming he "stamps the footage with realism in appearance and performance."

Overland Stage Raiders

RELEASE 1938
DIRECTOR GEORGE SHERMAN

DUKE'S STONY BROOKE and his fellow Mesquiteers combat Eastern gangsters who hijack a plane carrying gold shipments.

Overland Stage Raiders is the final picture to feature silent film icon Louise Brooks.

Olin Frances and John Wayne in *Overland Stage Raiders* (1938).

Santa Fe Stampede shot at the Iverson Movie Ranch in Chatsworth, California.

Santa Fe Stampede

RELEASE 1938
DIRECTOR GEORGE SHERMAN

AFTER THE MESQUITEERS' partner Carson (William Farnum) finds gold, the corrupt mayor Gil Byron (LeRoy Mason) has him killed. To make matters worse, Byron has his crooked sheriff arrest John Wayne's Stony Brooke, falsely accusing him of the murder.

Red River Range

RELEASE 1938
DIRECTOR GEORGE SHERMAN

As part of the Mesquiteers' investigation of a notorious gang of cattle rustlers, Duke's Stony Brooke manages to infiltrate the group by claiming to be an outlaw named Killer Madigan. According to Lorna Gray, who plays Jane Mason in the film, John Wayne was also thinking a step ahead behind the scenes. While shooting a scene on a porch, Gray recalled, the star intentionally tripped over a nail multiple times, requiring several takes until the extras on set qualified for overtime pay.

Second from left: Max Terhune, Dick Rush (with badge), Ray Corrigan (standing hat in hand), LeRoy Mason, Tom London, John Wayne and Ferris Taylor (with gavel) in *Santa Fe Stampede* (1938).

John Wayne and Stanley Blystone in *Red River Range* (1938).

Max Terhune, John Wayne, Ray Corrigan, Martin Spellman and Genee Hall in *Santa Fe Stampede* (1938).

Stagecoach

RELEASE 1939
DIRECTOR JOHN FORD

WHEN MOVIEGOERS in 1939 first saw John Wayne as Ringo Kid, they witnessed an actor finally fulfilling his cinematic potential. The character's introductory scene begins with the crack of a rifle shot and (what is now) a familiar voice blending stern authority with youthful exuberance shouting, "Hold it!" The camera cuts to John Wayne as Ringo Kid, in the prime of his life, ready to write his own legend. He then expertly twirls his Winchester rifle in a gesture that broadcasts the absolute confidence of both character and actor before the camera zooms in on Duke, focusing on the face that would soon become synonymous with the Western genre. It's a scene that captures the appeal of Duke as a movie star like never before, and one that still remains a go-to example of the actor's unique charisma.

It was an introduction that almost never came to pass. After the box office failings of *The Big Trail* (1930), Duke spent most of the 1930s working in low-budget Westerns and adventure serials, honing his natural talent into a more professional craft. According to the legend's own unpublished memoir, director and mentor John Ford casually asked Duke in 1938 whom he should cast in the lead role for his upcoming film, *Stagecoach*. John Wayne, with typical humility, suggested Lloyd Nolan, a solid performer also known for starring in B-Westerns. "Hell, Duke, can't you play it?" Ford countered, according to Michael Goldman's book *John Wayne: The Genuine Article*. And just like that, after nine years of being stuck in the minor leagues of the movie business, John Wayne finally found himself with a real opportunity to hit out of the park and achieve A-list stardom.

That decade of craft-honing would certainly come in handy when John Wayne joined a cast as talented as the one bringing *Stagecoach* to life. This included Claire Trevor as Dallas, a lady

1

of ill repute with a heart of gold; Thomas Mitchell as the booze-soaked Doc Boone; George Bancroft as the put-upon lawman Marshal Curley Wilcox and John Carradine as Hatfield, the Southern dandy gambler. While these characters may have seemed like familiar archetypes of the genre (even back then), Ford knew he could trust the actors to present these tropes in ways that would still feel fresh and exciting for the audience. And even though he wasn't quite as proven as some of his seasoned castmates, John

1. John Wayne as Ringo Kid in *Stagecoach* (1939). **2.** Duke in a scene from the film. **3.** A poster for the film.

4

Wayne had no trouble providing the lion's share of fresh excitement as the somewhat mysterious hero who's hellbent on finding the men who murdered his brother and sent him to prison.

But for all the thrills provided by Ringo Kid's quest for vengeance, his romance with Dallas and various entertaining interactions between the characters on their journey to Lordsburg, *Stagecoach* simply wouldn't be the Western benchmark it is today without one of its most vital stars: Monument Valley. A vast stretch of 91,696 acres spanning the states of Utah and Arizona, the desert setting's breathtaking beauty

5

4. Andy Devine, George Bancroft, John Carradine, Donald Meek, Louise Platt (in feathered hat), Claire Trevor and John Wayne in *Stagecoach*. **5.** Yakima Canutt doubling for Duke during a stunt.

"There are some things a man just can't run away from."

—JOHN WAYNE AS RINGO KID

★ ★ ★

6. From left: George Bancroft, John Wayne and Andy Devine in *Stagecoach*. 7. A one sheet for the film. 8. Claire Trevor and John Wayne in *Stagecoach*. 9. From left: John Wayne, director John Ford and Andy Devine on the set of the film.

provided the film an epic backdrop that so many now associate with the genuine Old West. For decades to come, Ford and Duke would repeatedly return to Monument Valley, establishing the location as an essential component for crafting a Western classic.

When asked about his body of work on *The Glen Campbell Goodtime Hour* in 1971, Duke replied with a half-smile, "The good ones started with *Stagecoach*." And while no one could have fully predicted the incredible trajectory of the cinema star's career, the film did make critics take note of his superstar potential. As the *Hollywood Spectator* wrote in its review, "John Wayne seemed born for the part he plays." Decades later, author J.A. Place's book *The Western Films of John Ford* noted the legend's evident natural ability and uncanny charisma in the early role: "John Wayne immediately registers his star quality in the closeup, and we are drawn to him irresistibly." All these years later, that irresistible draw still hasn't worn off.

John Wayne in
Stagecoach (1939).

John Wayne in
New Frontier (1939).

HONING HIS CRAFT

Though *Stagecoach* made him a star, John Wayne refused to coast and instead spent the 1940s sharpening his acting skills.

Duke in *The Night Riders* (1939).

The Night Riders

RELEASE 1939
DIRECTOR GEORGE SHERMAN

AFTER JOHN WAYNE set a new standard for himself as Ringo Kid in *Stagecoach* (1939), he saddled up as Stony Brooke once again to deliver another stellar entry in the *Three Mesquiteers* series. When a fake Spanish nobleman wields a forged land grant to evict the Mesquiteers and many others from their ranches, the trio don disguises and steal from the land thief's collectors to give the money back to the ranchers.

The film's working titles were *Heroes of the Desert* and *Lone Star Bullets*.

Three Texas Steers

RELEASE 1939
DIRECTOR GEORGE SHERMAN

THIS *THREE MESQUITEERS* film features Carole Landis as Nancy Evans, a circus owner betrayed by her partners, who try to swindle her into selling her ranch. When she protests by going to live at the property instead, her neighbors, the Three Mesquiteers, become her protectors. *Variety* praised Duke's performance in the film, noting, "Wayne hits the top with first-rate riding and carries his teammates along at a fast clip throughout."

Wyoming Outlaw

RELEASE 1939
DIRECTOR GEORGE SHERMAN

A POOR MAN named Will Parker (Don "Red" Barry) steals a steer from the Mesquiteers in order to feed his family. Rather than retaliate, the trio instead decide to help the man and his family stand up to a corrupt politician making his life increasingly difficult.

New Frontier

RELEASE 1939
DIRECTOR GEORGE SHERMAN

AFTER BEING HELD hostage by corrupt politician William Proctor (Harrison Greene), the Mesquiteers escape in time to have a chance at stopping an irrigation system from intentionally flooding a residential valley. Coming out on the winning side of a fierce battle that ensues, Stony manages to shut down the floodwaters in the nick of time. *The Film Daily* wrote that Duke's final Mesquiteers entry "stacks up with the better Westerns," adding, "Wayne in his cool style does a fine job."

Allegheny Uprising

RELEASE 1939
DIRECTOR WILLIAM A. SEITER

IN 1759, the British authorities are dead-set on making an unsavory trade deal in Pennsylvania's Allegheny Valley, and after trying tirelessly, Smith and his crew ditch the idea of debating their way to stopping the deal and instead focus on taking action. With painted faces and loaded rifles, Smith and his men saddle up and prepare to carry out their plan to ambush a wagon train carrying military supplies. Just as the men are about to ride into action, though, Jim discovers that one of them is not a man at all but in fact his fiery girlfriend, Janie (Claire Trevor), fully disguised like the others.

Claire Trevor and John Wayne in *Allegheny Uprising* (1939).

"I guess you Brits will never understand our ways."

—JOHN WAYNE AS JIM SMITH

★ ★ ★

1

Dark Command

RELEASE 1940
DIRECTOR RAOUL WALSH

I N 1940, with his big break officially under his belt, John Wayne looked to continue his momentum by teaming up with the director who gave him his first opportunity to star in a major motion picture 10 years prior, Raoul Walsh. Though their first outing suffered at the box office due to the Great Depression, the duo were undeterred and ready to prove their collaborative chemistry was no fluke the first time. And with the addition of a few more familiar faces on set, John Wayne was poised to keep his star rising with *Dark Command*.

Duke's co-stars in *Dark Command* also provided a distinct advantage, ensuring the film's success. Playing his love interest was Claire Trevor, with whom the actor had already displayed major chemistry in both *Stagecoach* and *Allegheny Uprising* in 1939. Also joining the cast was George "Gabby" Hayes, a man the legend had spent much of the 1930s with in B-Westerns including *Riders of Destiny* (1933) and *The Man from Utah* (1934). And before he became a household name via the likes of *My Pal Trigger* (1946) and his beloved TV series, Roy Rogers lent additional cowboy credibility to *Dark Command*, marking the only occasion in which he and Duke crossed paths on the big screen.

The film sees John Wayne as Bob Seton, a Texan who ventures to Lawrence, Kansas, alongside dentist Doc Grunch (George Hayes) and soon finds himself running for marshal against school teacher William Cantrell (Walter Pidgeon). Seton is quickly smitten with local Mary McCloud (Claire Trevor) and hopes that winning the race will also win him Mary's hand.

After befriending her brother Fletch (Roy Rogers), Seton manages an upset victory, causing Cantrell to spiral out of control and rally a group of raiders to wreak havoc. As Cantrell's nefarious faction grows, Marshal Seton is left with no choice but to create his own militia with the townspeople who won't let Lawrence go down without a fight.

While it's not typically remembered as one of the must-see films from John Wayne's iconic career, *Dark Command* still managed to emerge from the giant shadow cast by *Stagecoach* the year prior. Duke was undoubtedly on a mission to prove that his riveting role as Ringo Kid was no fluke, and in the eyes of critics, he did just that. *The New York Times* wrote in its review, "The most pleasant surprise of the picture is the solid performance of John Wayne as the marshal... Mr. Wayne knows the type, and given a character to build, he does it with vigor, cool confidence and a casual wit."

1. Walter Pidgeon, John Wayne and Claire Trevor in a scene from *Dark Command* (1940).
2. An insert for the film.

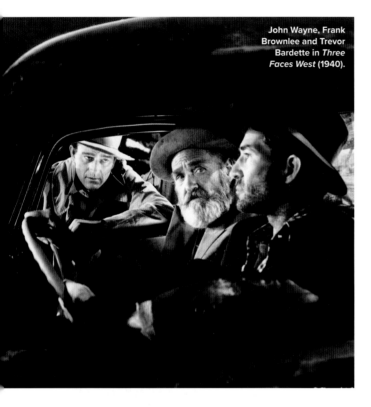

John Wayne, Frank Brownlee and Trevor Bardette in *Three Faces West* (1940).

Three Faces West

RELEASE 1940
DIRECTOR BERNARD VORHAUS

WHEN DR. KARL BRAUN (Charles Coburn) and his daughter Leni (Sigrid Gurie) arrive in a small North Dakota town seeking refuge from Hitler, things become complicated for Duke's John Phillips. Dust Bowl winds force Phillips to lead his fellow townspeople to Oregon, and he ends up developing strong feelings for Leni along the way. Trouble is, Leni is engaged to the man who helped her and Dr. Braun escape the Third Reich.

The Long Voyage Home

RELEASE 1940
DIRECTOR JOHN FORD

BASED ON FOUR separate Eugene O'Neill plays, this film sees John Wayne's Olsen and his fellow crew members on a merchant ship struggle to stay sane as they battle loneliness, monotony and uncertainty with smuggled booze and women. Critically injured following a storm that takes a toll on the ship, sailor Yank (Ward Bond) tries to give Olsen a wake-up call by telling him that a life spent stuck at sea is no life at all.

Dating back to their USC football days, the real friendship between John Wayne and Ward Bond adds a deeper layer of emotional weight to the film.

Seven Sinners

RELEASE 1940
DIRECTOR TAY GARNETT

THE FIRST OF four on-screen pairings of John Wayne and scene-stealer Marlene Dietrich has Duke playing Navy officer Lt. Dan Brent stationed on a fictional South Pacific island where Dietrich's Bijou Blanche sings at a nightclub. Lt. Brent and Blanche naturally fall in love and undergo several adventures involving magicians, antagonistic nightclub owners, deserters and more. The chemistry between Dietrich and Duke coupled with the exotic locale makes for a captivating romance that still holds up against any other example of the genre today.

Duke and Ward Bond in *A Man Betrayed* (1941).

In the final scene of *A Man Betrayed*, a policeman carries a package that reads "The End."

A Man Betrayed

RELEASE 1941
DIRECTOR JOHN H. AUER

WHEN HIS FRIEND is shot and killed at a nightclub called The Inferno in Temple City, John Wayne's small-town lawyer Lynn Hollister leaves his rural surroundings to investigate the scene of the crime himself. Hollister begins to put the pieces together when he learns that the club's illegal gambling ring is run by corrupt politician "Boss" Tom Cameron (Edward Ellis), but the ambitious lawyer gets himself tangled in the web when he meets and falls for Cameron's daughter, Sabra (Frances Dee).

*"Missed you?
I can't work,
can't think,
can't even
read a report!"*

—JOHN WAYNE AS JOHN REYNOLDS

★ ★ ★

Lady from Louisiana

RELEASE **1941**
DIRECTOR **BERNARD VORHAUS**

IN THIS SOUTHERN-FRIED romantic drama from *Three Faces West* (1940) director Bernard Vorhaus, John Wayne stars as John Reynolds, a crusading lawyer investigating the suspected rigging of a 19th-century lottery in The Big Easy. Filled with themes of corruption and greed and topped off with a pair of star-crossed lovers, the film's imaginative tale and fish-out-of-water role for Duke make it an early standout in the legend's extensive career.

The Shepherd of the Hills

RELEASE **1941**
DIRECTOR **HENRY HATHAWAY**

UNDER THE DIRECTION of Henry Hathaway—who would direct Duke in his Oscar-winning role in *True Grit* (1969) decades later—John Wayne turned in a memorable performance as the brooding Matt Matthews in this Midwestern drama. An Ozark Mountain moonshiner, Matthews is obsessed with finding and killing the father he never knew, who abandoned Matthews's recently deceased mother. Eventually, Matthews does come face to face with his father, who turns out to be the town's beloved newcomer Daniel Howitt (Harry Carey).

In addition to the weight of a father-son conflict, the casting is particularly significant given John Wayne's admiration of Harry Carey. The actor served as a major influence on Duke, who credits Carey with inspiring him to pursue the grittier type of cowboy character he would come to perfect throughout his career.

In the eyes of critics, John Wayne had already learned a lot in his young career by the release of *The Shepherd of the Hills*. *Variety* wrote that Duke "handles himself with exceptional ability as the young Ozarkian," while the *Motion Picture Herald* raved, "The entire cast is excellent, with top honors going to John Wayne for his top job to date."

John Wayne in *The Shepherd of the Hills* (1941).

John Wayne and
Joan Blondell in *Lady
for a Night* (1942).

"...a well-made picture program of considerable mass appeal."

—*MOTION PICTURE EXHIBITOR*

★ ★ ★

Lady for a Night

RELEASE 1942
DIRECTOR LEIGH JASON

THE EARLY 1940s were a unique time in John Wayne's career. Still a newly-proven leading man at that point, it seemed some studio executives wanted to see who else Duke could be on the big screen besides a rifle-toting cowboy. With 1942's *Lady for a Night*, the star proved he could play the part of a lovesick aristocrat just as well as he could spin a Winchester.

Duke's Jack Morgan co-owns the *Memphis Belle* riverboat casino with Jenny Blake (Joan Blondell), with whom he'd love to be more than business partners. Jenny, however, out to improve her reputation around town, decides to spontaneously marry a poor plantation owner and forgive his gambling debt. As Morgan's romantic dreams go up in smoke, so does the *Memphis Belle*, leading Duke's protagonist on a journey full of dramatic twists, turns and deceitful deeds until he finally gets a true chance with Jenny. Commending all aspects of the drama, *Motion Picture Herald* wrote that the film is "directed with skill and feeling," adding, "There is much of charm, warmth and appeal in the telling of the story."

Reap the Wild Wind

RELEASE 1942
DIRECTOR CECIL B. DeMILLE

O N THE HANDFUL of occasions in which John Wayne stepped outside of the Western and war genres, moviegoers always walked away with a greater appreciation for the actor's talents. A case in point would be this atypical period piece, a rip-roaring seafaring picture that still entertains thanks to Duke's unbeatable charisma. The timing of the film's release certainly helped its success at the time, arriving after Duke's breakout role in *Stagecoach* (1939) but before he became such an overwhelming presence in theaters that some audiences had trouble seeing him as an actor first and star second. The role of Jack Stuart, a ship's captain who commits some morally questionable acts in his quest for love and glory, probably wouldn't have been taken by John Wayne later in his career. But before studios became intensely focused on promoting Duke's image as an unambiguous hero, the actor was game for an interesting change of pace—which is exactly what he got with this unique adventure flick.

Reap the Wild Wind's setting also makes it an interesting early outlier in Duke's filmography. Taking place during the 1840s, the movie's action centers on the Florida Keys and follows the fortunes of Loxi Claiborne (Paulette Goddard) and the two men vying for her heart. Loxi runs a salvage company with the honorable intention of saving the crew and cargo of any merchant ships floundering on the Keys' treacherous reefs. This puts her in stark contrast to the regally named King Cutler (Raymond Massey) and his younger brother Dan (Robert Preston, prior to becoming better known to modern audiences as Harold Hill in 1962's *The Music Man*), who conspire with unscrupulous crew members to purposely wreck ships in order to collect their cargo. The Cutlers' latest

"If I thought that wreck was planned,
I'd make a topsail out of Cutler's hide!"

—JOHN WAYNE AS CAPT. JACK STUART

target is the Jubilee, captained by Duke's Jack Stuart, who was knocked unconscious by a treacherous shipmate and left powerless to stop the Jubilee from crashing against the reef. The Cutlers plunder the ship's cargo while Loxi saves the crew, subsequently losing her heart to the handsome sailor while he is convalescing at her home in the Keys. Jack returns Loxi's affections and confesses to her his greatest ambitions in life are to take over the Charleston shipping company he works for and then to take her hand in marriage. The headstrong Loxi, already heading to Charleston to visit her aunt, sees an

opportunity to help her lover by seducing his company rival, the foppish but capable Stephen Tolliver (Ray Milland). In the end, Stuart betrays his own sense of honor by purposefully wrecking a ship to gain advantage over Tolliver, but he redeems himself by sacrificing his own life for his rival's in an improbable but spectacular underwater battle against a vicious giant squid.

The complex plot avoids descending into convolution thanks to the strong performances of all the leads and the expansive vision of producer and director Cecil B. DeMille. DeMille was one of the first directors to establish himself in the burgeoning motion picture industry decades before *Reap the Wild Wind*, helming groundbreaking films such as *The Ten Commandments* (1923), *The King of Kings* (1927) and *Cleopatra* (1934). With this picture, the aging DeMille

1. John Wayne in *Reap the Wild Wind* (1942).
2. Paulette Goddard and John Wayne in *Reap the Wild Wind*. **3.** A pea coat worn by Duke in the film.
4. A promotional six-sheet for the film.

proved he hadn't lost his touch for creating epic tableaus that immediately draw audiences into the scene, whether it's the deck of a ship under assault from the rage of an ocean storm or the pastoral paradise of a Charleston plantation. "Mr. DeMille and his writers plot a picture very carefully for scenic effects," reads the *New York Times* review of the film. "And, in this particular instance, they have favored themselves magnificently. 'Reap the Wild Wind' bulges with backgrounds which have the texture of museum displays. Rooms reek of quality and substance, gardens look like the annual flower show, and the scenes of ships on the high seas exude a definite suggestion of salt air. The gentleman spends money on his pictures. Dollar signs are distinguishable everywhere."

5. Ray Milland and John Wayne in *Reap the Wild Wind*.
6. A *Reap the Wild Wind* comic. **7.** John Wayne, Ray Milland, Robert Preston and Raymond Massey in a scene from the film. **8.** Ray Milland, Lynne Overman, Paulette Goddard and John Wayne in *Reap the Wild Wind*.

While the film is known today as a "John Wayne movie," one of *Reap the Wild Wind*'s surprising delights is the chemistry between actors Goddard, Milland and Duke. Goddard manages through a forceful, honest performance to convince audiences her duplicitous and independent Southern belle is more than just a poor man's Scarlett O'Hara. And Milland successfully balances the tightrope with his character between silliness (Stephen Tolliver decides employing an amateur ventriloquist act using his lap dog is the best way to flirt with Loxi) and seriousness. But Duke's performance is the one that stands the test of time. The role of Jack Stuart gives Duke the opportunity to play an ambitious young striver, a tender lover and a guilt-ridden criminal all at once, and the rising star satisfies on all accounts. It's a performance any fan of the legend will treasure, and it's proof that one of Hollywood's great actors has plenty to offer audiences beyond the beloved classics.

Randolph Scott, Marlene Dietrich and John Wayne in *The Spoilers* (1942).

Edgar Kennedy, Emmett Lynn and John Wayne in *In Old California* (1942).

The Spoilers

RELEASE 1942
DIRECTOR RAY ENRIGHT

IN EARLY 1900S Nome, Alaska, Duke's Roy Glennister looks to cash in on a gold mine he's laid claim to. But before he can seal the deal, Glennister discovers that the crooked gold commissioner Alexander McNamara (Randolph Scott) has stolen the mine right out from under him. A standout scene sees Glennister confronting the commissioner in the saloon after learning of his dastardly deed, which naturally leads to the two men brawling all over the bar. The patrons look on in amusement as the miner and the commissioner fight it out, and Glennister even goes crashing through a window at one point, sending shards of glass flying through the air. *Variety* called special attention to the climactic fight in its review, writing, "The slugging match in the final reel between Wayne and Scott is apparently something that could be staged profitably at Madison Square Garden. It is that spectacular."

"You take a band of angry men defending their homes, mix well and serve hot."

—JOHN WAYNE AS TOM CRAIG

★ ★ ★

In Old California

RELEASE 1942
DIRECTOR WILLIAM C. MCGANN

JOHN WAYNE STARS as Tom Craig, a Boston pharmacist who relocates his business to Sacramento, California, only to be framed by corrupt politician Britt Dawson (Albert Dekker), who makes it appear as though Craig is selling poisoned drugs. When Dawson and his crew begin attacking local homes next, Craig leads a group of locals to retaliate against the outlaws. The role likely hit close to home at times, as Duke's father, Clyde Morrison, worked as a pharmacist after moving the family to Glendale, California.

John Wayne, Paul Kelly
and John Carroll in
Flying Tigers (1942).

Flying Tigers

RELEASE 1942
DIRECTOR DAVID MILLER

BEING THE COMMANDER of the flyboys as a global conflict unfolds means John Wayne's Captain Jim Gordon has to make plenty of tough decisions—and that only becomes more apparent when pilot Woody Jason (John Carroll) joins the crew. The two men are old friends, but their relationship quickly becomes complicated by Woody's ego-driven, brash behavior. Rather than following orders and working within the unit, the young pilot would rather go into business himself, creating a reckless environment in the process. When it becomes clear Woody is not only a danger to himself but also the Flying Tigers as a whole, Gordon realizes he has to put his past with the pilot aside and fire Woody for the greater good of the mission.

Flying Tigers was Duke's first World War II film, and it gave a promising preview of the conflict-inspired drama the actor would deliver to audiences for years to come. *The New York Times* called the film "a first-rate aerial circus chock-full of exciting dogfights", adding, "Mr. Wayne is the sort of fellow who inspires confidence."

"Where do you think you are, with some broken-down flying circus?"

—JOHN WAYNE AS CAPT. JIM GORDON

★ ★ ★

Randolph Scott and
John Wayne in *Pittsburgh*
(1942). Inset: Duke and
Marlene Dietrich on set.

Pittsburgh

RELEASE 1942
DIRECTOR LEWIS SEILER

AIMING TO SHOOT straight to the top of the Pittsburgh steel industry,
John Wayne's Charles "Pittsburgh" Markham prioritizes his career over all
the important people in his life. Though he achieves financial success, he
quickly realizes that he's left everyone he loves at the wayside. But just as
it looks like he's hit a personal rock bottom, it appears he may get a second
chance to make things right.

Joan Crawford, John Wayne and Henry Daniell in *Reunion in France* (1942).

Ava Gardner appears briefly as a fashion salon worker in *Reunion in France.*

Reunion in France

RELEASE 1942
DIRECTOR JULES DASSIN

BEFORE JOHN WAYNE'S war films became the grittier, succeed-at-all-costs narratives that would win endless praise for their realism, the star occasionally found himself as the man in uniform who unexpectedly finds love on the battlefield. In this film from director Jules Dassin, Duke plays Pat Talbot, a Royal Air Force bomber pilot whose plane goes down in Nazi-occupied Paris. He's discovered and brought to safety by Michele de la Becque (Joan Crawford), who, after being disenchanted by her lover's German ties, decides to smuggle Talbot to Portugal.

John Wayne and Jean Arthur in *A Lady Takes a Chance* (1943).

Duke in a publicity photo for *In Old Oklahoma* (1943).

True Grit (1969) director Henry Hathaway was initially slated to helm the film before William A. Seiter came on board.

A Lady Takes a Chance

RELEASE 1943
DIRECTOR WILLIAM A. SEITER

NEW YORKER Molly Truesdale (Jean Arthur) flees boredom in the Big Apple—as well as her three suitors—for a bus tour of the West. In a classic meet-cute moment, she comes face-to-face with free-spirited rodeo star Duke Hudkins (John Wayne), who shows the city slicker a thing or two about love in the Wild West. John Wayne's unmatched masculine charm makes what could be a tired rom-com an entertaining romp that can still melt hearts.

In Old Oklahoma

RELEASE 1943
DIRECTOR ALBERT S. ROGELL

THIS WESTERN FROM filmmaker Albert S. Rogell showcases the very best in excitement and suspense without sacrificing romance for climactic, explosive action. Duke stars as Daniel Somers, a cowboy battling it out with greedy oilman Jim "Hunk" Gardner (Albert Dekker) over oil lease rights on Native American land. And when the beautiful schoolteacher Catherine Allen (Martha Scott) comes along, the two men end up competing for her heart as well. *The New York Times* had high praise for Duke's performance, writing, "Mr. Wayne, as usual, is as convincing as a knockout punch."

John Wayne on the set of *In Old Oklahoma* (1943).

The Fighting Seabees

RELEASE 1944
DIRECTOR EDWARD LUDWIG

DUKE LIVED A long, rich life filled with countless triumphs (and even a few failures), but if historians had to point to one event that defined Duke's place in history, World War II would certainly rank high. Given John Wayne would become a living symbol of the country he loved, it's small wonder the conflict that radically altered the United States also reshaped the course of his career. Following the attack on Pearl Harbor, moviegoers expected more from Hollywood than mere entertainment—they craved uplifting stories to help ease the doubt and fear they felt as the world plunged into violent chaos. Fortunately, they had John Wayne waiting in the wings, the very model of strength, dignity and hope for a better future.

Duke first dabbled in the subject of the war in 1942's *Flying Tigers*, but 1944's *The Fighting Seabees* would fully focus on the conflict that was consuming the country's hearts and minds. The film strives to accomplish more than just featuring a few scenes of American soldiers routing Japanese troops—it tells the story of a group of skilled but stubborn civilians who painfully learn the necessity of militarization and discipline, a lesson millions could relate to by the time of the film's release. Duke plays Wedge Donovan, the head of a construction crew responsible for helping the Navy construct airstrips, bases and anything else the military needed to occupy and fortify the Pacific islands. The beginning of the film sees Donovan clashing with Lt. Cmdr. Robert Yarrow (Dennis O'Keefe) over the Navy's refusal to arm his construction crew, who are unable to defend themselves against attacks by the Japanese. Yarrow and Donovan quickly agree on the unsustainability of the status quo but differ on how to solve the problem—Yarrow

JOHN WAYNE
SUSAN HAYWARD
in

ROMANCE OF THE SEVEN SEAS

The Fighting Seabees

with DENNIS O'KEEFE
LEONID KINSKEY
WILLIAM FRAWLEY
GRANT WITHERS
J. M. KERRIGAN
EDWARD LUDWIG Director
Second Unit Directed by HOWARD LYDECKER and AENEAS MacKENZIE
Screenplay by BORDEN CHASE
Original Story by BORDEN CHASE

A REPUBLIC PICTURE

wants to form a battalion of construction workers under the auspices of the Navy, while Donovan balks at the length of time it would take for his men to complete training. Complicating matters between the two men is a shared affection for journalist Constance Chesley (Susan Hayward), who can't decide for much of the movie whether she should remain true to her beau Yarrow or follow her passion into the arms of Donovan. After a Japanese attack leaves much of Donovan's crew (and Constance) wounded, the hot-headed construction boss realizes the error of his ways and supports Yarrow's efforts to form a construction battalion, called the Seabees. Now strictly by-the-book, Donovan leads the battalion with model discipline and valor, going so far as to sacrifice himself during another battle against the Japanese in order to secure victory for the Navy.

Republic Pictures poured $1.5 million into the production of *The Fighting Seabees*, making the patriotic film a major endeavor for a

1. John Wayne and J.M. Kerrigan in *The Fighting Seabees* (1944).
2. An insert for the film. **3.** John Wayne, Dennis O'Keefe and Susan Hayward in *The Fighting Seabees*.

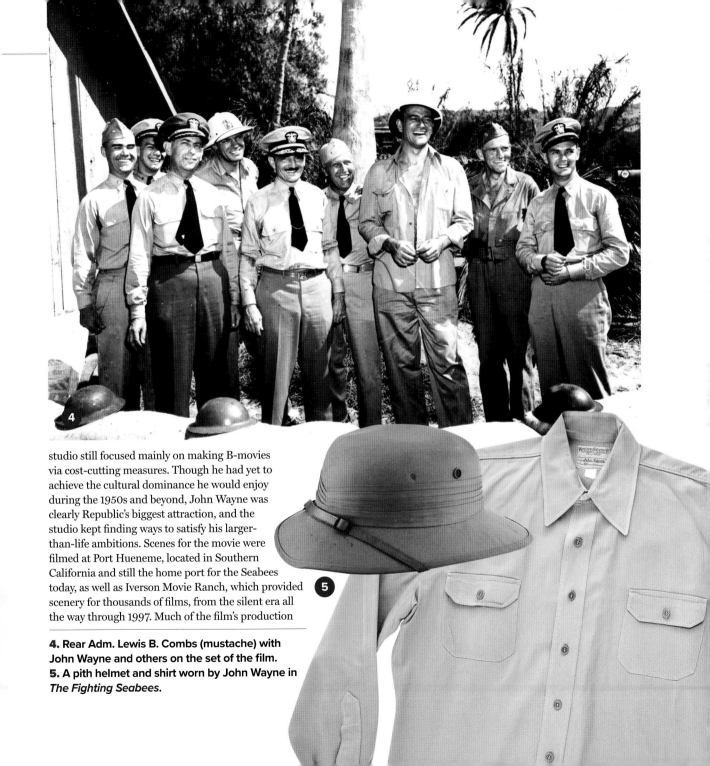

studio still focused mainly on making B-movies via cost-cutting measures. Though he had yet to achieve the cultural dominance he would enjoy during the 1950s and beyond, John Wayne was clearly Republic's biggest attraction, and the studio kept finding ways to satisfy his larger-than-life ambitions. Scenes for the movie were filmed at Port Hueneme, located in Southern California and still the home port for the Seabees today, as well as Iverson Movie Ranch, which provided scenery for thousands of films, from the silent era all the way through 1997. Much of the film's production

4. Rear Adm. Lewis B. Combs (mustache) with John Wayne and others on the set of the film.
5. A pith helmet and shirt worn by John Wayne in *The Fighting Seabees*.

budget went into transforming the Southern California landscape into the hellscape of the Pacific Islands during wartime, complete with fake palm trees and plenty of pyrotechnics to simulate the explosive mortar attacks and air raids of the Japanese.

For audiences both at the time of the film's release and today, the most important takeaways of *The Fighting Seabees* aren't found in its scenes of warfare, but in the emotional honesty presented in the moments in between them. The film never shies away from showing the tragic aftermath of battle, even one ending in victory for the good guys. Duke's character slowly realizing that his selfishness has no place in the fight for freedom is a lesson that remains just as vital today, making the role one of the most poignant in John Wayne's career.

6. Dennis O'Keefe and John Wayne in *The Fighting Seabees*. **7.** John Wayne (center) in a scene from the film. **8.** A pressbook for *The Fighting Seabees*. **9.** Foreground from left, starting with pith helmet: William Frawley, J.M. Kerrigan, Susan Hayward, John Wayne and Grant Withers in a scene.

"I was wrong, rotten wrong and everything."

—JOHN WAYNE AS WEDGE DONOVAN

John Wayne (left) in *The Fighting Seabees* (1944).

Tall in the Saddle

RELEASE 1944
DIRECTOR EDWIN L. MARIN

JOHN WAYNE ONCE famously pondered, "If everything isn't black and white, I say, 'Why the hell not?'" These words often define the appeal of Duke's on-screen image: a man wielding an unwavering handle on what's right and wrong and a willingness to follow his moral code no matter how tough the road ahead. It's also one of the reasons why *Tall in the Saddle* (1944), which at first glance might seem like just another entertaining John Wayne Western, remains such a fascinating entry in the icon's filmography. Directed by Edwin L. Marin and produced by Robert Fellows for RKO Radio Pictures, the film throws John Wayne and all of his moral convictions in the middle of a plot filled with an assortment of shady characters worthy of the most cynical film noir. Duke's character provides the contrast needed to make his exploits in the seedy Arizona town of Santa Inez that much more interesting, and it makes *Tall in the Saddle* a hidden gem within the silver screen star's incredible career.

Given the popularity of detective films at the time, noir conventions were bound to start cropping up in other genres. The original story for *Tall in the Saddle* was penned by Gordon Ray Young as a novel serialized in the *Saturday Evening Post* from March 7 to April 25, 1942, when writers such as Dashiell Hammett and Raymond Chandler were seeing their mystery novels adapted to the big screen with big success. Producer Robert Fellows (who would later form an independent production company with Duke) went on to enter a business relationship with Mickey Spillane, author of the Mike Hammer novels.

Perhaps bowing to the prevailing winds of noir blowing through Tinseltown, the film sees John Wayne as Rocklin, a strapping young ranch hand who arrives in the town of Santa Inez with the promise of employment at the K.C. Ranch only to find the owner has been murdered. At every turn along

1

the way, Rocklin finds himself embroiled in the conflicting agendas of Santa Inez's residents, from the smooth-talking lawyer Robert Garvey (Ward Bond) to the hot-headed gambler Clint Harolday (Russell Wade) and his equally short-tempered, gun-toting sister Arly (Ella Raines). Everyone wants something from Rocklin, but nobody is forthcoming, and the newcomer only has his physical capabilities and grit to depend on. The plot takes a bevy of twists and turns, with Rocklin being framed for the murder of Harolday, then uncovering a plot between Garvey and Harolday's stepfather (a powerful rancher in his own right) to dispossess the area's ranchers of their land and sell it for a profit to farmers. In the end, Rocklin brings justice to the town and gets his girl (in

this case, there's some tension as to whether Rocklin will end up with Arly or the sweet-spoken Easterner he shared the stagecoach to town with, another nod to the Western's film noir influence).

With so many evolving plot points to follow, much of the audience's enjoyment of the film rests on Duke's shoulders. Vignettes such as Harolday robbing an unarmed Rocklin of a poker pot, only to cave when Rocklin returns a few minutes later with his gun, underscore the point that Duke's

1. Paul Fix, John Wayne, George "Gabby" Hayes and Raymond Hatton in *Tall in the Saddle* (1944). **2.** John Wayne, Frank Puglia and Ella Raines in the film. **3.** Duke, Frank Orth and Ward Bond in *Tall in the Saddle*.

character is not to be disrespected. Similarly, scenes such as Arly taking shots at Rocklin in the street while he does his best to ignore the bullets, striding into a saloon and nervously ordering a whiskey, show a somewhat vulnerable—and even a comedic—side to John Wayne. Helping these scenes shine to their full potential is a cast of masterful supporting actors such as Paul Fix (who also co-wrote the screenplay), Harry Woods and George "Gabby" Hayes as the drunken but loyal stagecoach driver Dave.

The New York Times summed up the film's critical reception at the time of its release: "This is a regulation rough-and-tumble Western. Everything happens just as it did twenty years ago, starting with a thundering stage-coach ride through the hills of the sagebrush country and ending with the customary romantic clinch. In between there are furious fist fights, shootin' frays and much panting from hard-ridden horses... Just take 'Tall in the Saddle' for what it is, a rousing old-fashioned Western, and you won't go wrong." It's by no means a scathing take on the film, but one that overlooks both its joys and its bold blending of film tropes from different genres. Among the dozens and dozens of underseen John Wayne Westerns, *Tall in the Saddle* deserves to be placed near the top of the list.

4. Ella Raines and John Wayne in *Tall in the Saddle*.
5. From left: John Wayne, Gabby Hayes, Ward Bond and Emory Parnell in a scene from the film.
6. A promotional one sheet for *Tall in the Saddle*.

"Wayne is at his best in the type of role he plays here."

—THE HOLLYWOOD REPORTER

John Wayne
and Ella Raines
in *Tall in the
Saddle* (1944).

Flame of Barbary Coast

RELEASE 1945
DIRECTOR JOSEPH KANE

WHILE HE DID carve out a 50-year career as an inspiring icon of manliness, John Wayne had few on-screen opportunities to truly display his knack for suave, smooth-talking. In 1945's *Flame of Barbary Coast*, though, the star would approach the character of Duke Fergus with a low-key cool that still resonates today.

Arriving in San Francisco to collect a debt from crooked gambler Tito, Montana cowboy Duke Fergus makes it clear he holds all the cards. Now a skilled gambler, Fergus scores a big win that earns him the moniker "The King of Luck" from the flirtatious Flaxen (Ann Dvorak). As he links arms and walks off with the woman, he tells her, "The name's Duke, lady."

The icon's quietly charismatic portrayal of Duke Fergus was not lost on critics. *Variety* wrote that John Wayne "handles himself very well in the role of the man from the plains," while *The Los Angeles Examiner*'s review states, "Wayne, as usual, is sturdy, steady and solid as the breezy man from the West." Rare as it was to describe one of his roles in such a way, John Wayne's turn as Duke Fergus proved he was more than capable of engaging in heavier material with a lighter touch.

Several real American POWs appear at the end of the film thanks to the U.S. military's cooperation with executive producer Robert Fellows.

Back to Bataan

RELEASE 1945
DIRECTOR EDWARD DMYTRYK

RELEASED ONLY A few years after the battle for which it's named, 1945's *Back to Bataan* soars thanks to its favoring of a truthful depiction of the conflict rather than a Hollywood reimagining. While John Wayne's character (Colonel Joseph Madden) is technically fictional, he was largely inspired by Colonel George S. Clarke, the film's technical advisor who commanded the 57th Infantry Regiment of the Philippine Scouts.

In order to inject more historical accuracy, the script underwent several rewrites before it was finally deemed an honorable depiction. The result is a gritty telling of the aftermath of the fall of the Philippines to the Japanese, focusing on Col. Madden and Anthony Quinn's Captain Andrés Bonifácio organizing the local resistance to employ complex guerrilla tactics against the invaders. In the end, *Back to Bataan*'s message to audiences is unmistakable as Madden tells a Filipino child, "You're the guy we're fighting this war for."

That sentiment—as well as the film's historical accuracy—struck a chord with critics. *The New York Daily News* called the film "one of the best pictures of the war," and noted that "its realistic presentation ... gives it an authority that many war films ... lacked."

John Wayne in *Back to Bataan* (1945).

Vera Ralston and John Wayne in *Dakota* (1945).

Dakota

RELEASE 1945
DIRECTOR JOSEPH KANE

BETWEEN HIS PAIR of World War II films focusing on the defense efforts of the Philippines against invading Japanese forces, John Wayne returned to form with this exciting oater not unlike the kind he frequently starred in a decade prior. The actor stars as professional gambler John Devlin, who marries Sandy Poli (Vera Ralston), the daughter of prominent railroad tycoon Marko Poli (Hugo Haas). Soon after becoming a member of the wealthy family, Devlin finds himself entangled in a plot between land-grabbing industrialists and honest farmers who are fighting to keep their crops and property.

Helmed by Joseph Kane, who worked with John Wayne on *Flame of Barbary Coast* (1945) as well *The Lawless Nineties* (1936) a decade earlier, *Dakota* is a well-crafted Western that satiated fans of Duke's work in the genre as the actor ventured into more war films. Praising the pleasingly natural action of the film, *The New York Times* noted John Wayne's very capable hands, writing, "[T]he producers also give the hero plenty of opportunity to bowl over the badmen with his bare fists."

They Were Expendable

RELEASE 1945
DIRECTOR JOHN FORD

CONTINUING THE MISSION that began with *Back to Bataan*, Duke's 1945 film *They Were Expendable* depicts U.S. efforts to help the Philippines defend against the Japanese during World War II. This time, the focus would be on the real-life heroism of the Motor Torpedo Boat Squadron Three, an outsized unit of Navy PT boats that fought off Japanese invaders. Lending the film the perspective of real military personnel were Navy veteran Ernest Saftig, who served as technical advisor, and U.S. Marines Captain James C. Havens, who worked as second unit director.

For all its thrilling sea battles and the undeniable chemistry of co-stars John Wayne as Lieutenant "Rusty" Ryan and Robert Montgomery as Lieutenant John Brickley, the film succeeds most in delivering heartfelt moments. At a makeshift funeral for two fallen members of his crew, Duke's Ryan eulogizes the men, "Squarehead" Larsen (Harry Tenbrook) and "Slug" Mahan (Murray Alper), calling Larsen "the best cook in the Navy" and even reciting a bit of poetry for Mahan, whom Ryan recalls was "always quoting verse." Performances like this one are the reason General Douglas MacArthur would later compliment Duke's stirring portrayals of American servicemen on the silver screen.

> *"In war, you gotta forget those things and get buried the best way you can."*
>
> **—JOHN WAYNE AS LIEUTENANT "RUSTY" RYAN**

★ ★ ★

From left: Paul Langton, Robert Montgomery, Jeff York, John Wayne and Marshall Thompson in *They Were Expendable* (1945).

Without Reservations

RELEASE 1946
DIRECTOR MERVYN LEROY

THOUGH ON PAPER, it appears to be another film featuring John Wayne as a stoic man in uniform, *Without Reservations* is a film capable of reminding audiences that things aren't always as they seem on the surface. Claudette Colbert's Kit Madden is a renowned author whose struggle to adapt one of her books into a film only becomes more challenging once she falls for John Wayne's dashing Marine pilot Captain Rusty Thomas on a fateful train ride. After Cary Grant falls through as the film's lead, Madden can't help but feel Capt. Thomas has come into her life as the man meant to fill the role. As Capt. Thomas reads the book and finds plenty to dislike, though, Madden becomes fearful of how the captain will react and decides to hide the fact that she is the famous author behind it. Eventually, after hitting it off on some misadventures that follow their unceremonious ejection from the train, Capt. Thomas learns Madden's true identity and determines she's been using him in hopes that he'll agree to star in the film.

The nuanced characterization of Duke's Capt. Thomas was welcome at a time when leading men were usually playing heroic he-men who dismissed the types of feelings that drive the central conflict of *Without Reservations*. *Hollywood Reporter* believed the star had never been more natural, writing, "[T]he performance delivered by John Wayne as the Marine captain is the easiest of his career."

Angel and the Badman

RELEASE 1947
DIRECTOR JAMES EDWARD GRANT

WITH ALL THE skill he displayed on both sides of the camera, even a true John Wayne fan would be forgiven for thinking *Angel and the Badman* was released much later in the legend's career than 1947.

After a scuffle that leaves him badly wounded, Duke's notorious gunman Quirt Evans is brought to the home of a Quaker family and nursed back to health. Evans's affinity for massive breakfast feasts and his uniquely affable charm make him a welcome guest to the family, who disregard the others in town who try to warn them of the outlaw's reputation. Evans falls for the daughter, Penelope (Gail Russell), and even suggests he'll adopt the non-violent Quaker lifestyle in exchange for her hand in marriage. But after the re-emergence of Laredo Stevens (Bruce Cabot), the man who murdered his foster father, Evans appears prone to falling back into his old ways when he struggles to fight his thirst for vengeance.

Serving as a test drive for his new production company, John Wayne Productions, *Angel and the Badman* was Duke's debut in the producer's chair. Recognizing the actor's first time coordinating behind-the-scenes aspects of a film, *Time* praised Duke in its review: "John Wayne, whose first production it is, has dared to make a genteel Western. What is more remarkable, he has gotten away with it."

> *"Funny thing about pancakes: I lose my appetite for 'em after the first couple o' dozen."*
>
> **—JOHN WAYNE AS QUIRT EVANS**

★ ★ ★

John Wayne, Harry Carey and Gail Russell in *Angel and the Badman* (1947).

John Wayne (center) in *Tycoon* (1947).

During production, the film's working title was In the Darkness of the Sun.

Tycoon

RELEASE 1947
DIRECTOR RICHARD WALLACE

THIS FILM SEES John Wayne trading the wide-open vistas of the American West for the jungles and tunnels of South America. Duke's Johnny Munroe works as a hot-shot engineer whose main concerns are building a tunnel through the Andes Mountains at the behest of his tin mogul employer and falling in love. The apple of his eye is Maura Alexander (Laraine Day), the daughter of his employer. In the climax of the film, a flash flood threatens to wipe out a half-finished bridge, giving the actor a chance to showcase his cinematic heroism—a quality he would display in spades for decades to come.

Fort Apache

RELEASE 1948
DIRECTOR JOHN FORD

THE FIRST ENTRY in director John Ford's Cavalry Trilogy, 1948's *Fort Apache* sees John Wayne as Captain Kirby York alongside Henry Fonda as Lieutenant Colonel Owen Thursday, whose arrogant approach to the cavalry's conflicts threatens to undermine Capt. York's more mindful one. Though York technically serves under Thursday at the Fort Apache post, the two continually clash like co-leaders vying for command, with the brash lieutenant's insensitivity toward the Apache being the main subject of York's scrutiny. After Duke's protagonist promises Apache leader Cochise (Miguel Inclán) peaceful talks if they return to American soil, Thursday decides that their troops will march against them instead. Standing strong against the callous Thursday, York declares that he gave his word to Cochise and he has every intention to keep it.

One of the more underexplored manifestations of the moral code of Wayne's characters, this act of called-for insubordination remains a particularly powerful standout. It's a leap from the negative and hateful stereotypes of Native Americans often shown on the silent screen, and John Wayne's commanding presence made him the perfect choice to deliver the progressive message loud and clear. Commending Duke's performance, *The New York Times* wrote, "John Wayne is powerful as his captain, forthright and exquisitely brave."

"No man is gonna make a liar out of me, sir."

—JOHN WAYNE AS CAPTAIN KIRBY YORK

★ ★ ★

John Wayne and Henry Fonda in *Fort Apache* (1948).

Red River

RELEASE 1948
DIRECTOR HOWARD HAWKS

BY 1948, THERE was no disputing John Wayne's status as a bona fide box office star—and more importantly to the studio heads, a box office draw. In the span of a decade, Duke managed to put a great deal of distance between himself and the minor B-picture movies he made as an up-and-coming actor, which gave him a degree of freedom to take the reins and shape his career. And in true Duke fashion, he didn't rest on his laurels. John Wayne always sought to challenge himself by taking on new roles that spoke to his true character behind the scenes. With the character of Thomas Dunson in director Howard Hawks's *Red River*, the actor found a canvas upon which he could paint one of the most well-rounded arguments for the importance of values ever committed to film.

Dunson isn't a white hat-wearing congenial cowboy who rides into town with a smile and a quick draw to clear out the bad guys, kiss the girl and head off into the sunset. He's a man who often acts like a tyrant to his employees and ruthlessly marches straight into what appears to be a fatal fight with his adopted adult son. "He creates a larger-than-life character made human, and therefore sympathetic, through his flaws," says Brian Eggert, head critic of the film website *Deep Focus Reviews*. "What Wayne was willing to do more than many heroic actors of his day was portray characters wounded in some way or another." The story of how this wounded character copes with his beliefs and values when they're tested to their extremes makes *Red River* the ultimate "John Wayne values" movie.

Much of the credit for *Red River*'s strong statement about personal character can be given to director Howard Hawks, who often gravitated toward stories about codes of living, particularly when it came to the idea of the self-made man. Films such as 1932's *Scarface* and 1941's *Sergeant York* tackled the idea of how an individual can

1. John Wayne (on horse) in *Red River* (1948). 2. John Wayne dukes it out in a scene from the film. 3. A *Red River* insert. 4. A script for the film.

achieve greatness (or notoriety, in the case of *Scarface*'s Tony Camonte) through strength of will. It's no surprise Hawks would return time and again to the Western genre, where an individual's tenacity and grit not only shape their life but also the budding civilization depicted in those films.

Red River's plot centers on a cattle drive led by Duke's Dunson, a man whose only family is his adopted son Matt Garth, played by Montgomery Clift. Dunson, Garth and a gang of hired hands traverse treacherous terrain on their way from Texas to Missouri, the threat of starvation looming over every step after a stampede and other assorted disasters leave them short on supplies. Dunson's harsh measures to enforce discipline on the trail include whipping one of his employees and attempting to lynch two more who deserted the group, taking with them a sack of flour. "In reality, cattle drivers like Dunson needed to be hard and unflinching, sometimes even cruel, to survive," Eggert says. "They made tough decisions and, much as Dunson does, created their own rule of law." Dunson's responsibilities as a leader of men dictate that he take what he considers to be necessary measures, even as Garth deems those measures an unacceptable violation of the bond between the makeshift family comprised of the men on the trail. Unwilling to endure the menacing methods any longer, Garth leads the crew in booting Dunson from the cattle drive. Blind with rage, Dunson vows to kill the young man he once considered a son. After tracking down Garth, who has taken control of the cattle drive and guided them to Abilene, Kansas, Dunson initiates a no-holds-barred brawl—but fortunately, it isn't a fight to the death. The two men reconcile, delivering a statement about how even when

our values pull us in conflicting directions, they'll see us through our most trying moments.

Unlike any part John Wayne had played before, the complex character of Thomas Dunson made an impact on audiences. *The New York Times* felt the star had given one of his best performances, writing, "This consistently able portrayer of two-fisted, two-gunned outdoor men surpasses himself in this picture. We wouldn't want to tangle with him." Arriving at a pivotal point in his career, *Red River* was proof that despite his consistent portrayals of infallible Western heroes, John Wayne was not to be pigeonholed.

5. Walter Brennan, Mickey Kuhn and John Wayne in a scene from *Red River*.
6. John Wayne and Joanne Dru in a scene from *Red River*.

1

3 Godfathers

RELEASE 1948
DIRECTOR JOHN FORD

TYPICALLY CAST AS the man bringing the criminals to justice, John Wayne rarely played the likes of a cattle-rustling, bank-robbing outlaw. And in a Western film, the bank robbers seldom turn out to be the heroes. But in 1948's *3 Godfathers*, the script was somewhat flipped when Duke played Robert Hightower, a charismatic crook who pulls off a heartwarming miracle through nothing but undying determination.

The film opens with Hightower and his cattle-rustling partners Pedro "Pete" Roca Fuerte (Pedro Armendáriz) and William Kearney (Harry Carey Jr.) robbing the bank in the small Arizona town of Welcome. During the trio's attempt to flee the town with their ill-gotten goods, Kearney receives a gunshot wound from an armed citizen. But the more grievous blow by far is dealt by town marshal Buck Sweet (Ward Bond), who punctures the outlaws' water bag with a bullet, making the trio's escape to the desert a potential death sentence. Battling the punishing heat, the three men make their way to a known source of fresh water in the desert, only to discover that the well has been inadvertently destroyed by a traveler. The outlaws also find the traveler's pregnant widow (Mildred Natwick) in a nearby wagon, and they help the woman deliver a baby boy. On the verge of death from the difficult childbirth, the mother uses her last words to ask the bank robbers to see her son to safety. Following her passing, the three men make for the town of New Jerusalem, but their number dwindles down to just one after Kearney succumbs to his wound and Fuerte breaks his ankle in a prairie dog hole, forcing him to stay behind. Hightower staggers on with the infant in his arms, and just when it looks like the desert will claim him as well, a donkey appears and helps him traverse the remaining distance. Hightower arrives in town just in time for a

Christmas celebration, the newborn boy safe and sound as promised. When Sweet arrives soon after, he recommends the lightest sentence possible for the bank robber, who pledges to return after his release from prison to help raise the boy.

The themes of family and caring for your fellow man found in *3 Godfathers* were a perfect match for the behind-the-scenes crew and actors, many of whom had worked together for years. At the helm was John Ford, already a longtime friend and mentor to John Wayne. On screen, Duke got to make more memories with his old pal Ward Bond, while Harry Carey Jr. was undoubtedly thinking about the bond of family, as his father starred in a 1916 version of the same story. Ford counted the senior Harry Carey as one of his great

---

1. Harry Carey, Jr., John Wayne and Pedro Armendáriz in *3 Godfathers* (1948). **2.** John Wayne and Ward Bond (holding rifle) in the film. **3.** A *3 Godfathers* pressbook.

friends, but the director didn't let that affection prevent him from giving the tough love he was known for to his old pal's son—Carey Jr. would later describe Ford in his 1994 autobiography as "my nemesis and my hero." But underneath the legendary director's crabby exterior lay a softer side, as evidenced by a pre-credit sequence Ford shot that paid tribute to Harry Carey Sr., dedicating this version of *3 Godfathers* to his memory.

Duke, for his part, delivers a solid and believable performance as an outlaw who finds his conscience along with a newborn baby. "John Wayne as the leading badman and ultimate champion of the child is wonderfully raw and ructious," wrote Bosley Crowther for his review in *The New York Times*. When Duke's Hightower stumbles into the bar of New Jerusalem, baby in hand, and tells the bartender, "Set 'em up, mister. Milk for the infant and a cold beer for me," you don't doubt for a second he's going to get what he wants. That blend of humor, pathos and adventure marks *3 Godfathers* as a classic Ford and Duke outing best enjoyed around the holidays. With family, of course.

4. Behind the scenes on the set of *3 Godfathers*. **5.** John Wayne and John Ford between takes.

"Milk for the infant and a cold beer for me."

—JOHN WAYNE AS ROBERT HIGHTOWER

★ ★ ★

Wake of the Red Witch

RELEASE 1948
DIRECTOR EDWARD LUDWIG

BLINDED BY HIS quest for vengeance, John Wayne's Captain Ralls in 1948's *Wake of the Red Witch* eventually pays the price for his poor judgment. As captain of the *Red Witch*, Ralls is at odds with Mayrant Sidneye (Luther Adler), the owner of the vessel's shipping company. The rivalry revolves around a woman, Angelique (Gail Russell), whom Ralls feels was stolen away from him by Sidneye. In a reckless act of revenge, Ralls intentionally sinks the *Red Witch* and allows the millions of dollars worth of gold on board to plummet into the sea with it. The two men later agree on a deal to share the gold in exchange for Ralls's cooperation in recovering it, but the mission is revealed to be more perilous than previously understood. Ralls ends up being the only one willing to dive into the wreckage, and he is trapped by debris and drowns in the process.

Today, *Wake of the Red Witch* remains a fairly glaring standout in John Wayne's filmography. Not only does Duke play a rash fool who fails to course correct, his wrongheaded arrogance costs him his life—a fate rarely seen for any of the legend's characters. Noting the star's ability to step outside his comfort zone, *Los Angeles Examiner* wrote, "It is Wayne who carries the unusual film role of a sadistic hero. It's pretty strong stuff, and he makes it very convincing."

Duke's production company, Batjac, was named after the film's fictional shipping company, Batjak Limited.

She Wore a Yellow Ribbon

RELEASE 1949
DIRECTOR JOHN FORD

ANY TIME JOHN WAYNE and John Ford combined their massive talents, they reminded audiences just how capable they were of creating profound artistic statements about history, legacy and individualism. *She Wore a Yellow Ribbon*, Ford's 1949 middle entry of his Cavalry Trilogy, examines through the lens of Duke's Captain Nathan Brittles what it means to spend a life committed to an ideal and what becomes of that life when service is no longer required. "It's a film about maturity and old age," says Joseph McBride, film historian and author of *Searching for John Ford*. "Ford has always mourned the passage of time in his films."

In *She Wore a Yellow Ribbon*, the audience sees that passage literally marked by Capt. Brittles as the Cavalry officer counts the days down on his wall calendar to his mandatory retirement. It's 1876, and despite General Custer's crushing defeat at the Battle of Little Bighorn, the film takes place in a West that has been more or less won for settlers. Brittles receives orders to lead his troops on one last mission to deal with Native American warriors on the rampage following Custer's defeat. He also finds himself saddled with transporting his commanding officer's wife Abby Allshard (Mildred Natwick) and niece Olivia Dandridge (Joanne Dru) to a stagecoach where they'll flee to relative safety, a complication that creates tension among two of Brittles's junior officers competing for Olivia's affections.

At times, the film's plot borders on cryptic. "Ford disliked scenes with exposition, which forced the audience to use their intelligence to follow the plot," McBride says. But the soul of this classic is found in the scenes between Brittles and the men and women who have become family to him, such as Top Sergeant Quincannon (Victor McLaglen). Watching Brittles smell Quincannon's breath for the whiff of whiskey in the morning or

1

give a heartfelt talk about leadership to one of his younger officers establishes a history that makes Brittles's impending retirement that much more heart-wrenching. Inevitably, one of the most moving scenes of the film is when Brittles bids a fond farewell to his troops, revealing just how close he had grown to the men. And while credit should go to James Warner Bellah, who wrote the stories the script was based on, and screenwriters Frank S. Nugent and Laurence Stallings, the power of Brittles's pathos is owed to John Wayne's

performance. Although Duke was only in his early 40s while filming *She Wore a Yellow Ribbon*, he effortlessly exhibits the mixture of pride, regret and wisdom of a man decades older (an interesting showcase of Duke's acting abilities is to follow up a viewing of *She Wore a Yellow Ribbon* with the icon's final film, *The Shootist* (1976), to see how eerily accurate Duke was in his prediction of his own elderly mannerisms). The role of Nathan Brittles also allowed John Wayne to show a softer, gentler side to his persona. Scenes such as the one in which he talks to his deceased wife at her grave allow John Wayne to sink his teeth into one of the most well-rounded roles in his career.

1. John Wayne in *She Wore a Yellow Ribbon* (1949).
2. A shooting script for the film.
3. John Wayne reads the script for *She Wore a Yellow Ribbon*.

Though many believe Duke should have won an Academy Award for the role, the only person from *She Wore a Yellow Ribbon* who walked away with Oscar gold was cinematographer Winton C. Hoch. It's difficult to argue with the decision after watching how the gorgeous vistas of Monument Valley were captured for the movie, giving an epic scope to a personal story. For years after its theatrical run, the only surviving format of the film was in black-and-white, robbing audiences of one of the Technicolor era's greatest masterpieces (it wasn't until an effort spearheaded by UCLA that the film was restored to its vibrant colors).

4. John Wayne in *She Wore a Yellow Ribbon*.
5. Joanne Dru and John Wayne in *She Wore a Yellow Ribbon*.

"Yes, we are too old for war.
But old men should stop wars."

—JOHN WAYNE AS CAPT. NATHAN BRITTLES

★ ★ ★

Whether viewers today see the film in color or black and white, its emotional impact remains the same. Critics at the time considered *She Wore a Yellow Ribbon* to be one of Ford's finest films, as *Motion Picture Herald* wrote, "Not only a superb film in the western tradition but also one of the best efforts in John Ford's distinguished career." Decades later, Ted Sennett's 1990 book *Great Hollywood Westerns* praised John Wayne's performance, writing, "Playing a role older than his actual age, Wayne invested the character with a matchless strength and authority." Most importantly, the role would remain extremely meaningful to Duke for the rest of his life: While reflecting on his career during a 1971 appearance on *The Glen Campbell Goodtime Hour*, John Wayne referred to Capt. Nathan Brittles as "my favorite character."

6. John Agar, John Wayne, Harry Carey Jr. and Joanne Dru in *She Wore a Yellow Ribbon*. **7.** A half sheet for the film. **8.** Victor McLaglen and John Wayne in *She Wore a Yellow Ribbon*. **9.** John Wayne, John Ford and Ben Johnson on set.

John Wayne
on the set of
*The Fighting
Kentuckian* (1949).

The Fighting Kentuckian

RELEASE 1949
DIRECTOR GEORGE WAGGNER

STEPPING INTO THE role of a man just gutsy enough to stand up to powerful villains in defense of innocent civilians, John Wayne is right at home in 1949's *The Fighting Kentuckian*. In 1818 Alabama, Duke's militiaman John Breen uncovers a plot that would see land stolen right out from under a group of French settlers, including the woman he fancies, Fleurette De Marchand (Vera Ralston). But after being mistaken for a surveyor, Breen seizes the opportunity to spoil the dastardly plans by using his faux credentials to gain an upper hand. Finally, when the land-grabbing criminals arrive, Breen makes a valiant attempt to combat them. With Fleurette and his amusing partner Willie Paine (Oliver Hardy) by his side, Breen gives the greedy gang all he's got in the name of doing the right thing.

Impressed with his presence in the role of the courageous militiaman, *The New York Times* dubbed Duke, "handsome, laconic and a formidable lad with his fists and firearms." *Variety*, meanwhile, praised the star's ability to balance being both star and producer, a role he was still new to at the time, writing, "Wayne embarks here as a producer and does very well even if the camera constantly is on him."

"They're leavin', I'm stayin'!"

—JOHN WAYNE AS JOHN BREEN
(UPON MEETING FLEURETTE ON HIS MARCH HOME
AFTER FIVE YEARS OF SOLDIERING)

★ ★ ★

Duke and Oliver Hardy in *The Fighting Kentuckian* (1949).

Sands of Iwo Jima

RELEASE 1949
DIRECTOR ALLAN DWAN

WHILE JOHN WAYNE always aimed to entertain each time he stepped onto a set to craft another entry in his incredible filmography, a select few in Duke's career stand out as more than mere films and much more than entertainment. *Sands of Iwo Jima* (1949) manages to capture on celluloid the bravery, determination, despair, hope and sacrifice of the Marines who put it all on the line when their country needed them most. It isn't a movie: It's a memorial to the Greatest Generation and one that still manages to fill audiences with reverence and awe.

The idea for the film came to Republic Pictures producer Edmund Grainger while he was reading the newspaper one day. The phrase "sands of Iwo Jima" instantly leapt from the page, sparking a firestorm of creativity in the movie mogul's brain that quickly yielded a bare-bones plot outline: a strict Marine sergeant molds the men under his command into warriors able to withstand the horrors of combat. Grainger eventually landed a $1 million budget (the largest for any Republic movie at the time), and he wisely cast John Wayne in the starring role. The character of Sergeant John M. Stryker provided another high-profile opportunity for Duke to show a different side to audiences, who were becoming less likely to strictly view the star as a white hat-wearing cowboy thanks to his more complicated roles such as Thomas Dunson in *Red River* (1948) and Capt. Nathan Brittles in *She Wore a Yellow Ribbon* (1949) earlier that year. John Wayne's newfound pathos perfectly placed him to portray Stryker, a hard-as-nails Marine and natural leader whose personal life is in tatters. The stunning performance would earn him his first Academy Award nomination (though it would be another two decades before the legend would go home with the golden statue—see pg. 262).

1. Behind the scenes of *Sands of Iwo Jima* (1949).
2. Ira Hayes, John Bradley, John Wayne and Rene Gagnon in the film.

3. Richard Jaeckel, John Wayne, John Agar and Forrest Tucker in *Sands of Iwo Jima*.
4. Forrest Tucker, John Wayne, Allan Dwan, associate producer Edmund Grainger and Major General Graves Erskine on set.

Duke's spectacular on-screen work was surrounded by an equally impressive production. Republic Pictures had reached out to the Marine Corps in hopes of enlisting their support to create the most realistic World War II film to date. Grainger and director Allan Dwan didn't want to just make a war movie; they wanted to redefine the genre. The Marines, for their part, were discovering their most protracted battles weren't in the fields of France or the atolls of the South Pacific but in the windowless offices of Washington bureaucrats. Certain congressional and military leaders balked at the United States fielding two different land forces and campaigned to fold the Corps into the Army. As the Marines took stock of the Hollywood landscape, they determined movies glorifying their achievements were few and far between. They decided to throw the dedication and effort that liberated two continents into creating the greatest war story committed to film. Republic received full access to shoot at Camp Pendleton in California and was also granted use of a full battalion of Leathernecks to add to the film's epic scale.

Throwing in their planes, tanks, artillery, Jeeps and trucks for good measure, the Marines were determined to make the film's technical advisor Capt. Leonard Fribourg proud by giving the film as much authenticity as possible. The transformation of Camp Pendleton into the war-torn jungle of Iwo Jima was so complete and accurate, Gen. Holland M. Smith—who commanded the American forces at the real battle of Iwo Jima (and briefly played himself in the film)—remarked to reporters, "I felt as though I were back in the South Pacific. It's so real, it's almost frightening." The Marines even left the sets up after filming to use for training exercises.

But even with the full support and provided artillery from the real men in uniform, *Sands of Iwo Jima* could have been a blunder had the lead role been in the hands of a less-committed patriot. John Wayne's determination to honor America's heroes was palpable, and it was clear that critics had never seen anything quite like it. *The New York Times* raved: "Wayne is especially honest and convincing, for he manages to dominate a screen play which is crowded with exciting, sweeping battle sequences...There is so much savage realism in 'Sands of Iwo Jima'..." Honesty was always a badge of honor for John Wayne, and there was perhaps no other role he'd rather have such a word pinned to.

5. John Wayne on the set of *Sands of Iwo Jima*. **6.** A garrison cap and fatigues worn by John Wayne in *Sands of Iwo Jima*.

BECOMING AN ICON

By the 1950s, John Wayne was more than just a charismatic movie star—he was a symbol of American cinema itself.

John Wayne (left) in
Rio Grande (1950).

Rio Grande

John Ford agreed to make *Rio Grande* as long as Republic Studios allowed him to make *The Quiet Man*, which they thought would flop.

RELEASE 1950
DIRECTOR JOHN FORD

LIEUTENANT COLONEL KIRBY YORKE (John Wayne) is in the midst of a seemingly unwinnable battle in which Apaches are slaughtering settlers in the Southwest and then fleeing to restricted territory across the Rio Grande. To make matters worse, Lt. Col. Yorke must also deal with the surprise arrival of his estranged son Jeff (Claude Jarman Jr.), who is assigned to his command as a trooper. Soon after, Yorke's estranged wife, Kathleen (Maureen O'Hara), arrives at Fort Starke to insist Yorke discharge their son. The veteran Cavalry man scoffs at the idea, though, declaring to treat his son as he would any other trooper. His decision pays off as Jeff and his fellow troopers rescue a group of children taken hostage by the Apaches, which leads to Yorke reuniting with Kathleen as the two proudly watch their son receive honors for his heroism.

The final entry in John Ford's "Cavalry Trilogy," *Rio Grande* also marks the first time the trio of Ford, John Wayne and Maureen O'Hara all worked together. The three proved to be a winning combination for critics, as *Variety* called the film "outdoor action at its best, delivered in the John Ford manner," and praised the stars, writing, "Wayne is very good as the male star, and Miss O'Hara gives one of her best performances."

"He must learn that a man's word to anything, even his own destruction, is his honor."

—JOHN WAYNE AS LIEUTENANT COLONEL KIRBY YORKE

Operation Pacific

RELEASE 1951
DIRECTOR GEORGE WAGGNER

THE START OF the 1950s saw John Wayne returning to his Armed Forces film roots as Lieutenant Commander Duke Gifford, a member of the U.S. Navy fighting in World War II. Leading his submarine, the *Thunderfish*, on a rescue mission in the Pacific, Gifford welcomes aboard a group of nuns and orphans. When the *Thunderfish*'s torpedoes repeatedly malfunction in battle, the lieutenant commander makes it his mission to solve the problem himself and get everyone to safety.

Flying Leathernecks

RELEASE 1951
DIRECTOR NICHOLAS RAY

IN COMMAND OF the Wildcats, a unit of young Marine Corps aviators, John Wayne's Maj. Daniel Kirby butts heads with Capt. Carl Griffin (Robert Ryan) over the manner in which Kirby sends his men on deadly missions. With actual aerial war footage spliced into several scenes, the film is a particularly realistic look at the men who gave their lives fighting in the sky.

The Quiet Man

RELEASE 1952
DIRECTOR JOHN FORD

TWO DECADES INTO his big-screen career, John Wayne could have easily won a Hollywood superlative for "least likely to play a man who refuses to fight." But in 1952's *The Quiet Man*, Duke knew exactly what he had signed up for when he agreed to play the part of former boxer Sean Thornton. And as soon as the credits rolled, it was clear this romantic dramedy set in a sleepy Irish hamlet would be one of the defining films of his career.

After accidentally killing a man in the ring, prizefighter Sean Thornton returns to his birthplace, the Irish village of Innisfree, where he vows to live the rest of his life peacefully. Hoping to settle into his family's old cottage, Thornton inadvertently makes an enemy in notorious townsman Burly "Red" Will Danaher (Victor McLaglen), who had already planned on becoming the home's new owner. To make matters even more combustible between himself and Danaher, Thornton meets and falls in love with a woman named Mary Kate (Maureen O'Hara), who happens to be the antagonizing man's sister. Undeterred, the former fighter proceeds with his plans to acquire the cottage and take Mary Kate's hand in marriage. Danaher, however, attempts to derail the couple's future together by refusing to pay his sister's dowry. Finally, after calling Danaher out for his foul ways in front of the whole town, Thornton agrees to put his dukes

2

up. The two engage in a wild brawl that spills all over town, complete with mid-swing quips and cheers from the onlooking crowd of locals. Eventually, the two men land in a pub where they recognize a newfound respect for each other over a couple of pints.

Between Ford's signature style, the boiling conflict between John Wayne and Victor McLaglen's steadfast characters and the undeniable chemistry between Duke and Maureen O'Hara, *The Quiet Man* was a hit among critics. *Variety* showered the film with praise, particularly praising the efforts of Ford and Duke, writing: "Republic has an excellent money picture... It is a robust romantic drama... Wayne works well under Ford's direction, answering all demands of the vigorous, physical character." Meanwhile, *Look Magazine* simply stated that the film "should go down in history as one of the greatest comedies ever made."

1. Maureen O'Hara and Duke in *The Quiet Man* (1952). **2.** Barry Fitzgerald, John Wayne, Ward Bond and Victor McLaglen in the film. **3.** A cap worn by Duke for publicity photos. **4.** A one sheet for the film.

3

4

Joseph Stalin once ordered the KGB to assassinate Duke, but the plan was intercepted by the FBI.

Big Jim McLain

RELEASE 1952
DIRECTOR EDWARD LUDWIG

AN INVESTIGATOR FOR the U.S. House Un-American Activities Committee, Duke's Jim McLain heads to Hawaii to break up a ring of Communist Party members causing trouble in the Aloha State. Upon receiving news of their subpoenas, some of the conspiring communists decide to antagonize McLain, assuming he's unequipped to take them on by himself. Of course, this turns out to be a major mistake. Though vastly outnumbered, the tough-as-nails enforcer manages to hold his own in the film's chaotic brawls, leaving red, white and blue marks on the faces of the enemy and a lasting impression on viewers. Noting McLain's perfect casting, *Variety* dubbed John Wayne a "forceful hero" in its review, while *The Los Angeles Examiner* wrote, "John Wayne ... dominates [the film] as usual with his very personal appeal and charm."

Donna Reed, Vicki Raaf, John Wayne and Anitra Stevens in *Trouble Along the Way* (1953).

Trouble Along the Way

RELEASE 1953
DIRECTOR MICHAEL CURTIZ

THIS FILM FROM *Casablanca* (1942) director and occasional Duke collaborator Michael Curtiz sees John Wayne as Steve Williams, a formerly famous football coach desperate to do anything for custody of his daughter. As his ex-wife tries to paint him as an unfit father, Williams tries to raise his stock by taking a gig coaching football at a New York City college. When he realizes the team is in dire shape, Williams employs some shady recruitment methods to strengthen the roster, yielding an investigation that makes the fight for custody of his daughter even more of an uphill battle.

Island in the Sky

RELEASE 1953
DIRECTOR WILLIAM A. WELLMAN

THIS DISASTER FLICK sees John Wayne as the calm and collected Captain Dooley, a man facing the harrowing task of keeping a plane full of people alive after a crash in the freezing conditions of the Canadian wilderness. Using his resources wisely, the captain manages to keep the crew united in their mission to survive at all costs. Eventually, Dooley's patience and perseverance pay off as he's able to reach a rescue plane with a radio message.

Critics had no trouble believing Duke in the role of the inspiring survivalist character, as *Sign Magazine* wrote in its review, "Wayne is superb as a veteran pilot who subordinates his own worries and fears to concern for his men." *The Motion Picture Herald* called this "one of [Duke's] best performances."

John Wayne in *Island in the Sky* (1953).

Hondo

RELEASE 1953
DIRECTOR JOHN FARROW

WITH HIS PRODUCTION company Batjac up and running in the 1950s, John Wayne wanted to pool his resources to make a visually stunning 3D Western. At this point in his career, working behind the camera held as much interest to Duke as playing the role of leading man, and he was eager to shake things up by merely producing the film without also starring in it. Director John Farrow, a first-time collaborator for the star at the time, was tapped for the ambitious project, an adaptation of Louis L'Amour's novel about a cavalry dispatch officer protecting a mother and son from an impending battle between the Apache and the Army. Initially, Glenn Ford was tapped to don the iconic fringe shirt and cavalry hat, but a personality clash with Farrow caused the actor to drop out of the film, forcing Duke to step into Hondo's boots instead. Of course, the role was a natural fit, and audiences were treated to one of the most captivating characters of John Wayne's career.

The film follows Duke's Hondo Lane after having lost his horse in a hostile encounter with the Apache. He continues on foot accompanied by his loyal dog Sam (Pal), eventually arriving at the homestead of Angie Lowe (Geraldine Page) and her 6-year-old son, Johnny (Lee Aaker). After learning Angie's husband had abandoned his wife and child, Hondo decides to pitch in with the work that needs to be done around the house. In the process, he grows close to the family, and as he saddles up to leave (on a horse given to him by Angie), he asks the two to come with him. Despite knowing that tensions between the Apache and the settlers are about to come to a head, Angie refuses Hondo's offer, confident in her and Johnny's abilities to fend for themselves—especially since the young boy once stared down an Apache chief, who promised to leave the two alone as a result. Hondo reluctantly agrees to leave without

them, but on his ride away from the homestead, he runs straight into an ambush set by Angie's husband Ed (Leo Gordon), who recognizes Hondo's steed and takes him for a thief. Hondo kills Ed in self-defense, not realizing that he's Johnny's father until he finds a picture of the boy on Ed's corpse.

Though Hondo is rounded up by Apache raiders, he lucks out when Chief Vittorio (Michael Pate) finds the photo of Johnny on his person. Remembering his pledge not to harm Johnny and Angie, the chief releases Hondo. But the Apache's hot-headed second-in-command, Silva (Rodolfo Acosta), doesn't think this cavalry officer should get off easy after what the Army has done to his people. This results in a knife duel between the two. Hondo comes out on top but spares Silva's life. This act of mercy turns out to be a grave mistake as the ruthless Silva murders Hondo's dog. When the Apache haul a wounded Hondo to Angie's doorstep, believing him to be her husband, Angie goes along with the mistake in order to save the wounded cavalry man's life. As Hondo tries to lead Angie and Johnny safely out of the settlement, he is confronted by Silva, who has killed Chief Vittorio to become the new leader of the Apache. Hondo, fortunately, is quicker

1. Duke, Geraldine Page, Tom Irish and Ward Bond in *Hondo* (1953).
2. Duke in a scene from the film.

to the draw, and he blasts Silva away once and for all. As the Apache retreat to choose a new chief, Hondo, Angie and Johnny plan to make a new go of it in another town.

With its roller-coaster story that pushed the Western genre's boundaries, *Hondo* made a lasting impact. In his book *A Pictorial History of the Western Film*, William K. Everson called Hondo, "[P]robably the best John Wayne vehicle not made by John Ford." Duke's innate goodness casts the classic character in a sympathetic light as a flawed gunslinger trying to do the right thing, rather than a drifter seizing an opportunity with another man's wife. Geraldine Page, who had never starred in a feature film prior to *Hondo*, also made a big impression on audiences. The up-and-coming actress's performance impressed members of the Academy enough to be nominated for Best Supporting Actress. But behind Duke and Page's superb performances was the pen of James Edward Grant and his interpretation of L'Amour's story. Although his name might not ring as many bells as his legendary friend John Wayne, Grant was responsible for penning the scripts of many of Duke's classics, including *The Alamo* (1960) and *Donovan's Reef* (1963). Two other frequent collaborators in Duke's life also worked on the film: Ward Bond, who played Buffalo Baker, and *McLintock!* (1963) director Andrew V. McLaglen, who served as Unit Production Manager.

3. John Wayne, Ward Bond and James Arness on the set of *Hondo*. **4.** A mug gifted to the film's animal trainer Rudd Weatherwax. **5.** John Wayne between takes.

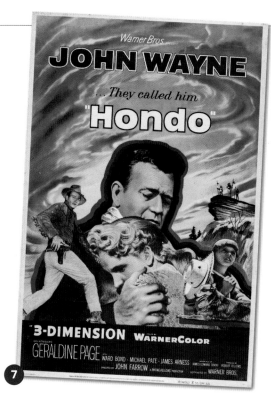

6. John Wayne in *Hondo*. 7. A rare 3D poster for *Hondo*. 8. John Wayne, Pal, Lee Aaker and Geraldine Page in a scene from the film. 9. Michael Wayne, John Wayne, Patrick Wayne and screenwriter James Edward Grant on location in Mexico.

"Everybody gets dead. It was his turn."

—JOHN WAYNE AS HONDO LANE

★ ★ ★

Perhaps the most interesting facet of *Hondo* from a film historian's point of view is how it was shot. At the time, 3D films were enjoying one of their sporadic moments in the sun, but not many Westerns ended up receiving the popular treatment. *Hondo*'s cinematographers, Robert Burks and Archie Stout, had quite a challenge shooting in the high heat of scenic Camargo, Mexico. Even Warner Bros. started to become disenchanted with the project and threatened to take away one of the special 3D cameras it

had lent to the production, but Duke stood by the film. He always prided himself on making a picture viewers could truly immerse themselves in and it paid off. "[T]he best 3-D movie to come out so far," a *Life* magazine reviewer wrote in its December 14, 1953 issue. "The film is beautifully photographed ... and with the added feature of depth will have theater audiences dodging spears, knives, horses, hatchets and Indians for whatever their lives are worth." Although viewers probably won't catch it in 3D today, *Hondo*, with its rolling, blistering desert, complicated characters and epic showdowns, still impresses as only a Duke classic can.

The High and the Mighty

RELEASE 1954
DIRECTOR WILLIAM A. WELLMAN

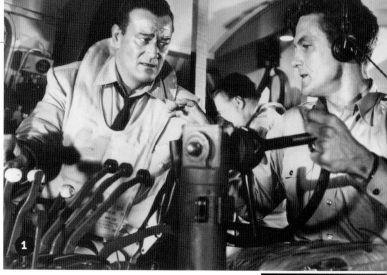

FROM FLOODS TO fires to bloodthirsty bandits, the types of danger Duke's heroes typically encountered would likely scare the life out of the average man. But fearlessness was a staple of the John Wayne persona, and for 1954's *The High and the Mighty*, the legend would take his portrayal of remarkable tranquility in the face of danger to new heights.

Appearing as part of the ensemble of passengers is Claire Trevor, with whom the legend lit up the screen in *Stagecoach* (1939) and *Dark Command* (1940). And at the helm of the film was William A. Wellman, the director Duke had worked with the year prior for *Island in the Sky* (1953), a film that coincidentally stars the icon as a captain dealing with the aftermath of a downed plane.

The High and the Mighty sees John Wayne as "Whistling" Dan Roman, a commercial airliner copilot who's often teased by the crew for being "old" and "washed up." But on a transpacific flight, Roman's years of experience come into play when the plane's mechanical problems appear dire and Captain "Skipper" Sullivan (Robert Stack) panics and plans to ditch. Haunted by a past crash, Roman slaps some sense into Sullivan and takes the helm. While not quite whistling in the face of danger, Roman is as calm and collected as anyone could be in such a terrifying situation. With the lives of numerous passengers at stake and hardly a drop of fuel to spare, he eventually determines they can indeed make it to a safe

"We're taking this bird all the way to Frisco."

—JOHN WAYNE AS DAN ROMAN

★ ★ ★

landing at the airport.

Naturally, Duke was completely convincing to critics in the role of the heroic copilot. *The New York Times* had particularly high praise for the legend, writing in its review, "John Wayne makes the best show as a veteran pilot, second in command, who has the coolness and courage to knock some clear sense into the muddled head of the captain." The role even earned the star the 1955 Golden Laurel Award from *Motion Picture Exhibitor* for Top Male Dramatic Performance—further proof that John Wayne could soar above and beyond the battlefields of World War II or the saloons of the Old West.

1. John Wayne and Robert Stack in *The High and the Mighty* (1954). **2.** Jan Sterling, David Brian, Claire Trevor and John Wayne in a scene from the film.

Lana Turner and John Wayne in *The Sea Chase* (1955).

While shooting *The Sea Chase*, John Wayne and Pilar Pallete spontaneously married against the Hawaiian backdrop. Director John Farrow gave the bride away.

The Sea Chase

RELEASE 1955
DIRECTOR JOHN FARROW

AS AN ANTI-NAZI German at the start of World War II in this film from *Hondo* (1953) director John Farrow, John Wayne's Captain Karl Ehrlich is a shining example of the type of stick-to-his-guns hero the legend is best known for. With the conflict expanding exponentially every day, Ehrlich has to think fast at all times. When his ship is low on materials to burn for fuel, he decides to take his chances with an escape rather than risk being sunk by his enemies and orders his crew to cut up the lifeboats to feed the vessel. The courageous captain's full-throated approach to all that he does is perhaps best revealed when Elsa (Lana Turner), the German spy he's transporting, asks him, "Have you ever in your life made a compromise with a conviction?" to which the captain replies, "I was always afraid that if I started, it wouldn't be easy to stop."

Praising the film's thrills, the *Motion Picture Herald* called *The Sea Chase* "a keen and suspenseful sea story of World War II," adding, "the picture is as handsome as it is full of action."

Lauren Bacall and John Wayne in *Blood Alley* (1955).

Blood Alley

RELEASE 1955
DIRECTOR WILLIAM A. WELLMAN, JOHN WAYNE (UNCREDITED)

NOT EVERY ACTOR can play a merchant Marine captain who breaks free from Communist capture without leaning on unrealistic action movie tropes, but Duke manages to do so with true believability in this seafaring adventure film produced by the legend himself.

After two years of imprisonment in a Chinese jail, Captain Tom Wilder finally escapes on a ramshackle boat with Chiku Shan villagers seeking refuge on board. Displaying impressive fortitude and survival instincts, he manages to navigate the decrepit vessel full of refugees all the way to Hong Kong, relying on nothing but his memory of the Chinese coast. In its review of the film, *Variety* noted the part of Capt. Tom Wilder is a call that could have only been answered by Duke, simply stating, "Wayne was a perfect choice to play the rugged skipper."

> ## "If you want a last look at home, you'd better take it now."
>
> **—DUKE AS CAPT. TOM WILDER**

★ ★ ★

The Conqueror

RELEASE 1956
DIRECTOR DICK POWELL

POSSIBLY THE MOST unique entry in John Wayne's entire filmography, this 1956 period epic stars Duke as Temujin, the Mongol chief who battled Tartar armies and rose to power as the notorious emperor Genghis Khan. Helmed by musical-comedy performer turned director Dick Powell, the film features the on-screen reunion of John Wayne and Susan Hayward, who previously co-starred in *Reap the Wild Wind* (1942) and *The Fighting Seabees* (1944).

The Searchers

RELEASE 1956
DIRECTOR JOHN FORD

N 1956, THE master crafter of the Western motion picture—John Ford—released his masterpiece, which also starred the physical embodiment of the Western spirit: John Wayne. Both men dedicated every ounce of their considerable talents and abilities to making *The Searchers*, a classic that's just as—if not more—revered for its cinematic accomplishments today as it was half a century ago. "There's so much depth of emotion in this film that there's no mistaking what John Ford and John Wayne both put into it," says film historian Leonard Maltin. "The movie deals with such fundamental emotions, and that gives the film so much power."

Based on a novel by Alan Le May and adapted to the screen by Frank S. Nugent, the film sees John Wayne as the troubled and nuanced Civil War veteran Ethan Edwards—a role that many consider to be the legend's greatest accomplishment as an actor. Edwards stands apart from his upstanding homesteader brother Aaron (Walter Coy) and his family, yet when a Comanche raid on the farm wipes out his kin with the exception of his adopted nephew Martin (Jeffrey Hunter) and his two nieces, Lucy (Pippa Scott) and Debbie (Lana Wood), who are missing, Edwards dedicates himself completely to finding the presumably kidnapped girls. *The Searchers* may seem like another story where the stoic, loner cowboy embarks on a righteous quest to protect his loved ones, but as Edwards's journey wears on and the bodies pile up, the character displays a dark side uncommon in most of Duke's movies. "You see the anger of the character, his hatred and desperation," says Maltin. "It's such a wide range of feelings." Even more disturbing, Edwards clearly intends to kill the grown Debbie (played by Natalie Wood) after believing she's "gone Comanche," a huge perversion in the former Confederate's eyes. Edwards's change of heart upon finally discovering

2

his niece, however, leads to one of the film's most emotional and legendary lines: "Let's go home, Debbie." In that moment, thanks to Duke's pitch-perfect delivery, the audience can hear the character let go of years of hate and revenge.

Underappreciated during its time, *The Searchers* slowly gained fans through the years and, in 1989, became one of the first films selected by the National Film Preservation Board as an American movie with strong cultural significance. The legacy of the Western also lives on through legendary filmmakers such as Martin Scorsese, George Lucas and Steven Spielberg, all of whom have cited the John Ford classic as an inspiration for their own work. The influence extends to the small screen as well, as Vince Gilligan, creator of the critically-acclaimed television drama *Breaking Bad*, said the film had a major influence on the final episode of the series. At that point

in the story, Bryan Cranston's megalomaniac drug kingpin Walter White is hellbent on killing his former partner Jesse Pinkman (Aaron Paul) at their next meeting. But once the two come face to face in the finale's heart-pounding climax, White spares Pinkman and even rescues him from his captors. "A lot of astute viewers who know their film history are going to say, 'It's the ending to *The Searchers*.' And indeed it is," Gilligan told *Entertainment Weekly*. "The ending of that movie just chokes you up, it's wonderful. In the writers room, we said, 'Hey, what about the *Searchers* ending?' So, it's always a matter of stealing from the best."

1. John Wayne in *The Searchers* (1956). **2.** John Qualen, Duke, Lana Wood, Ward Bond, Dorothy Jordan, Walter Coy and Robert Lyden in a scene. **3.** Duke in the film. **4.** Jeffrey Hunter, John Wayne and Harry Carey Jr. in a scene. **5.** A one sheet for *The Searchers*.

Though *The Searchers* was released more than six decades ago, time hasn't diminished John Wayne's most riveting and unforgettable role. "John Wayne is filmed as beautifully in that film as in anything he's ever done," rock icon Bruce Springsteen said while discussing the Western's influence during a 2019 interview with TCM. "*The Searchers* stood out as, I think, one of the greatest pictures ever made." Will there ever come a time when *The Searchers* doesn't hold some nugget of inspiration for aspiring artists? As Edwards himself would say, "That'll be the day!"

6. Duke and Ward Bond shooting a scene in Monument Valley. **7.** John Wayne and Natalie Wood in *The Searchers*. **8.** Clockwise: John Wayne, Jack Pennick, Jeffrey Hunter, Dolores Del Rio and John Ford on set.

John Wayne in *The Searchers* (1956).

The Wings of Eagles

RELEASE 1957
DIRECTOR JOHN FORD

BY THE LATE 1950s, John Wayne was well-versed in the role of the serviceman who sacrifices everything. In most of his World War II films, Duke portrayed fictional characters who were merely inspired by the real heroes who worked as consultants on his films. But with *The Wings of Eagles* in 1957, the star would find himself playing not only a real person but also a close friend of the film's director, John Ford. As Frank "Spig" Wead, John Wayne turned in a winning performance that explored the harsh reality so many men and women in uniform face: their careers in the Armed Forces being cut short.

While sympathetic to anyone with a beating heart, the story of the former Navy pilot who becomes paralyzed and unable to fly after a freak accident was particularly resonant with both Ford and Duke. Much like Wead, who turned to screenwriting after the accident halted his ability to fly, John Wayne only entered the film industry as a result of his college football career abruptly ending due to an injury. And having served in the Naval reserve as head of the Field Photographic Division in World War II, Ford, like Wead, was able to provide an invaluable perspective to the conflict-focused films he helmed. Together, the director and his most trusted leading man were well prepared to create a moving cinematic tribute to an inspiring figure.

When shooting began in Pensacola, Florida, in the summer of 1956, *The Wings of Eagles* was up against the challenges of a tight budget and a tighter schedule. Initially, MGM studios hoped to cut costs by modifying black-and-white stock footage to be used in much of the film. Ford's artistic acumen and determination to pay proper respects to his pal, however, would not allow such a shortcut. Still, the director had to work

3

2

with expert efficiency as he shot the film over the course of just 47 days. Fortunately, in addition to Duke, he had plenty of help from some of his most trusted stars— Maureen O'Hara plays Frank's wife Min Wead, while Ward Bond serves as John Dodge, a prickly Hollywood director crafted in Ford's own image. With the characters in capable hands and the studio's attempts to hinder the film's aesthetic thwarted, Ford could do the story justice.

The Wings of Eagles wastes no time establishing Frank "Spig" Wead's determined spirit. Prior to his accident, the vigorous U.S. Navy man is fiercely committed to the promotion of the Navy's flying program—a focus that gradually

1. John Ford and John Wayne on the set of *The Wings of Eagles* (1957).
2. Duke and Maureen O'Hara on set.
3. John Wayne and Dan Dailey in a scene from the film.

overshadows his personal life, including his relationship with his wife and children. But just as it appears Wead's career aspirations are about to ascend to the skies, he falls down a flight of stairs in his home and becomes a paraplegic. As he copes with his unfortunate new reality, Wead pursues screenwriting and soon sees some success. Still, refusing to remain permanently grounded, the flier works with his trainer "Jughead" Carson (Dan Dailey) to restore some of his mobility. In one of the film's most inspiring scenes, Carson has Wead repeat the phrase, "I'm gonna move that toe!" over and over again, commanding more vigor each time.

Hitting all the necessary notes of a

4. Duke and Dan Dailey in *The Wings of Eagles*. **5.** A custom mug given to Second Unit Director Edward O'Fearna. **6.** An insert for the film.

WHAT A GUY WAYNE!

M·G·M PRESENTS IN METROCOLOR

JOHN WAYNE
DAN DAILEY
MAUREEN O'HARA

The Wings Of Eagles

The life-inspired story of reckless, fun-loving, romantic "Spig" Wead, Squadron Commander.

WARD BOND

SCREEN PLAY BY FRANK FENTON AND WILLIAM WISTER HAINES
DIRECTED BY JOHN FORD PRODUCED BY CHARLES SCHNEE

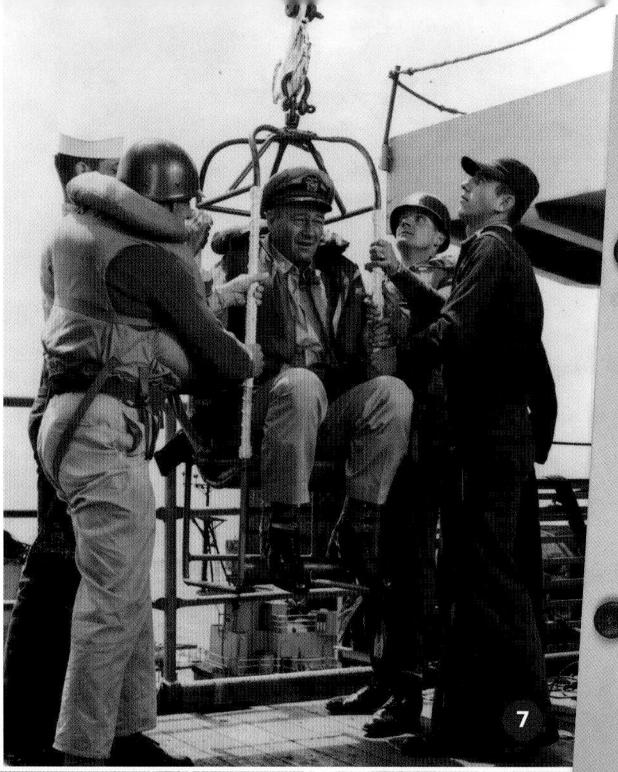

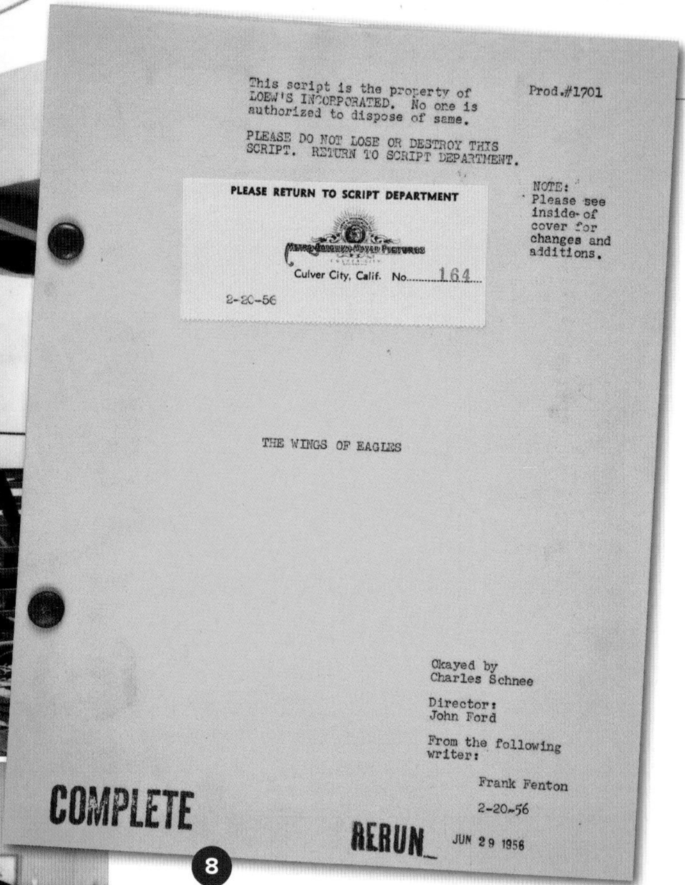

This script is the property of LOEW'S INCORPORATED. No one is authorized to dispose of same.

Prod.#1701

PLEASE DO NOT LOSE OR DESTROY THIS SCRIPT. RETURN TO SCRIPT DEPARTMENT.

PLEASE RETURN TO SCRIPT DEPARTMENT

Metro-Goldwyn-Mayer Pictures

Culver City, Calif. No. 164

2-20-56

NOTE: Please see inside of cover for changes and additions.

THE WINGS OF EAGLES

Okayed by Charles Schnee

Director: John Ford

From the following writer:

Frank Fenton

2-20-56

COMPLETE

RERUN JUN 29 1956

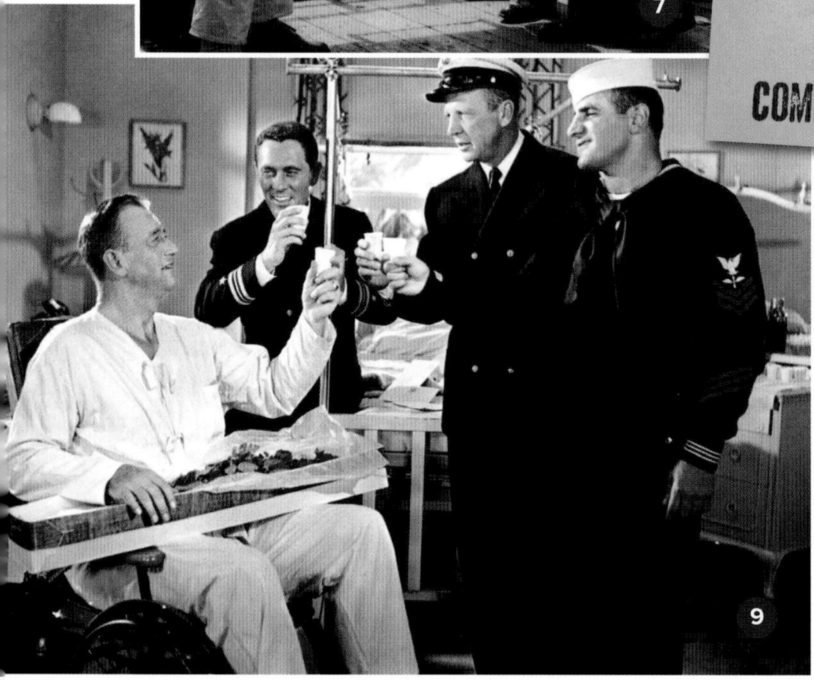

Hollywood smash while staying true to the story on which it's based, *The Wings of Eagles* was a soaring success. *Variety* called the film "an entertaining show with the thrills, action, heart and comedy that trademark nearly all of Ford's pictures," adding, "Wayne is particularly good as the vital man of action with a lust for life." Anyone who has ever fought to overcome obstacles and achieve their goals can likely relate to the story of Frank "Spig" Wead.

---

7. Duke on the set of *The Wings of Eagles*.
8. John Wayne's copy of the script.
9. From left: John Wayne, Ken Curtis, Dan Dailey and Tige Andrews in a scene from the film. 10. John Wayne on set.

The cast and crew of *The Wings of Eagles* (1957) pose with the crew of the *USS Philippine Sea*, the aircraft carrier featured in the film.

Janet Leigh and Duke in *Jet Pilot* (1957), which was produced by record-setting pilot Howard Hughes.

Jet Pilot

RELEASE 1957
DIRECTOR JOSEF VON STERNBERG

WHEN DUKE'S Air Force Colonel Jim Shannon and fellow officer Major Rexford (Paul Fix) investigate a Russian jet that has landed in Alaska, they are surprised to find the pilot is a woman seeking refuge named Lieutenant Anna Marladovna (Janet Leigh). Shannon is assigned to stick close to Anna in hopes that she'll give up Soviet secrets, but he winds up developing feelings for her. Later, when Anna is about to be deported, Shannon marries her. As it turns out, Anna is actually a Soviet spy named Olga sent to retrieve secrets from unwitting servicemen. But after the controversial newlyweds travel to Russia, Olga begins to realize her feelings for Shannon are legitimate.

Legend of the Lost

RELEASE 1957
DIRECTOR HENRY HATHAWAY

DUBBED A "[b]reathtaking adventure film"
by *The New York Daily News*, this 1957 picture
sees John Wayne as Joe January, an American
living in Timbuktu who's hired as a guide by Paul
Bonnard (Rossano Brazzi), an explorer searching
for the Lost City his father may have unearthed
years prior. As they set out on their journey,
unforeseen circumstances lead the two men to
join up with Dita (Sophia Loren), a prostitute
profoundly impressed by Paul's quest. But when
the expedition reveals ugly truths about Paul's
father, the explorer snaps and abandons Joe and
Dita in the desert with no supplies. Left with
only each other, the two fall in love as they fight
to survive and seek vengeance.

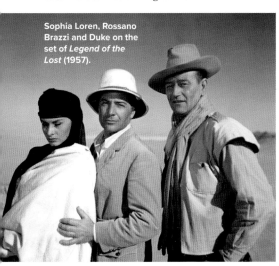

Sophia Loren, Rossano
Brazzi and Duke on the
set of *Legend of the
Lost* (1957).

I Married a Woman

RELEASE 1958
DIRECTOR HAL KANTER

PLAYING HIMSELF IN a cameo role, John Wayne's
appearance in this comedy from Hal Kanter serves as a plot
device that creates tension between its protagonists.
Stressing over an approaching deadline, advertising
executive Marshall Briggs (George Gobel) takes his
doting wife Janice (Diana Dors) to a fictional Technicolor
film called *Forever and Forever and Forever* starring
John Wayne and Angie Dickinson as meta versions of
themselves. Sure enough, seeing Duke on the big screen has
a profound effect on Janice as she watches the legend play a
passionate husband who puts his marriage before his work.

The Barbarian and the Geisha

RELEASE 1958
DIRECTOR JOHN HUSTON

FAR FROM THE vistas of Monument Valley, John Wayne
stars as Townsend Harris, the first U.S. consul to Japan, who
sails to the small fishing village of Shimoda in 1856. Soon
enough, Harris encounters hostility from the locals—except
for a lovely geisha, Okichi (Eiko Ando). Though the film
was quite unlike most others Duke starred in, *The New York
Herald Tribune* praised the star for allowing his signature
charisma to shine through, writing, "Even in a kimono, the
essential Wayne remains. His is a pleasant, unpretentious
and good-natured performance."

Rio Bravo

RELEASE 1959
DIRECTOR HOWARD HAWKS

THE STORY OF *Rio Bravo*, John Wayne and Howard Hawks's 1959 justice-and-redemption Western classic, begins with a simple reaction to a popular fad. Westerns had never been more in style than they were in late 1950s America. The tales of brave men and women conquering the wilderness appealed to a country increasingly comfortable in its position at the top of world politics. With the average American's horse and six-shooter replaced by a commuter train and briefcase, Westerns appealed to a nostalgic impulse. Echoing a sensibility that continues to this day, the birth of U.S. society in the West—with its white and black hats and its easily defined roles—was venerated as a "simpler" time. The escapism this love of the West provided at the box office was intoxicating, and the era produced some of the finest films in the genre thanks to this renewed interest.

As far as John Wayne and Howard Hawks were concerned, however, not all of the entries in this new wave of Westerns (the genre's first wave of massive popularity had come during the silent film era) were sending the right messages to their audiences. The Western's close ties to the birth of our nation as we know it, for Duke and Hawks, were something sacred. They believed the genre should enshrine what they saw as the best of American values—freedom, opportunity and, most of all, justice—in a way that was, if not explicit, then easily translatable to a mass audience. But other directors had disagreed at various points throughout the decade and made Westerns that seemed to fly in the face of everything Duke and Hawks loved about the genre. Fred Zinnemann's *High Noon* (1952) and *3:10 to Yuma* (1957), directed by Delmer Daves, were particular offenders.

High Noon is remembered by many as a classic in actor Gary Cooper's sterling career. But the plot sees Cooper's lawman ask everyone in town for help defeating an outlaw,

"Sorry don't get it done, Dude."

—JOHN WAYNE AS SHERIFF JOHN T. CHANCE

★ ★ ★

only to be turned away time and again, forced to face the outlaw alone. While some praised the departure from normal genre conventions, John Wayne thought otherwise. He publicly called the film "The most un-American thing I've ever seen." Old colleague Howard Hawks agreed, saying of the film, "I didn't think a good sheriff was going to go running around town like a chicken with his head off asking for help, and finally his Quaker wife had to save him." By the time *3:10 to Yuma* (1957) offered a similarly bleak and psychological take on the genre, Duke and Hawks were ready to launch their counter-offensive.

Along with screenwriters Leigh Brackett and Jules Furthman and a supporting cast including Angie Dickinson, teen sensation Ricky Nelson and future Rat-Packer Dean Martin, producer/director Hawks and his star set about resetting the Western genre in a mold of their own making—the story of Sheriff John T. Chance. Chance, played by Duke, is the kind of all-American lawman who embodies dignified strength in exactly the way Hawks and Duke felt characters in films like *High Noon* did not. When Chance, with the help of good-hearted local drunkard Dude (Dean Martin), arrests gunfighter Joe Burdette (Claude Akins) for shooting a man in a bar, their sense of justice is put to the test when Burdette's brother Nathan (John Russell) comes to town. Nathan makes it clear he's going to bust his brother out of jail, but Duke's Chance refuses to back down, enlisting Dude, a young cowboy called Colorado Ryan (Ricky Nelson) and an old man named Stumpy (Walter Brennan) to make a stand with him. As Chance's love interest, Feathers, Angie Dickinson plays

1. John Wayne and Ricky Nelson in *Rio Bravo* (1959). **2.** From left: Angie Dickinson, Dean Martin, John Wayne, Howard Hawks and script supervisor Meta Rebner on set. **3.** Duke and Angie Dickinson in a scene from the film.

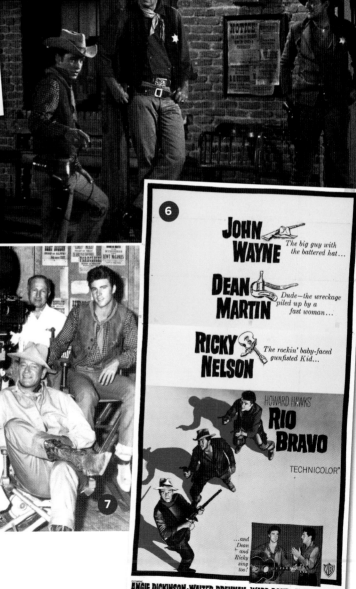

4. A document from Armada Productions signed by Duke and Howard Hawks. **5.** Ricky Nelson, Duke and Dean Martin in a scene. **6.** A *Rio Bravo* three sheet. **7.** Front from left: Dean Martin, Howard Hawks and Duke; second row: Walter Brennan, Russell Harlan and Ricky Nelson.

her character with just as much moral fortitude as Duke's, putting her in sharp contrast to the female characters in the kinds of Westerns Duke and Hawks wanted to discredit. As the small band of fighters face injury or death at the hands of the Burdette gang, they keep their sense of duty and justice. Even if it means the loss of their own lives, they are dedicated to bringing an end to the Burdettes' lawlessness once and for all. And most importantly, they do it together, with each contributing in his or her own way.

Chance champions a by-the-bootstraps individuality, but

---

8. Walter Brennan and John Wayne in *Rio Bravo*.
9. Duke, Howard Hawks and Angie Dickinson on set between takes **10.** John Wayne and Ward Bond in a scene from the film.

the film also recognizes the benefits of good people banding together. It was of the utmost importance to Howard Hawks and John Wayne that Western films, concerned as they were with the time period that made America the nation it became, argue for the values that helped the country achieve its size and influence rather than cast them into doubt. They were so concerned with telling stories like Chance's, in fact, that Hawks and Duke would team up for two more films that history has come to think of, along with *Rio Bravo*, as a trilogy. *El Dorado*, which was released in 1966, features Duke and Robert Mitchum playing a lawman/drunkard duo facing a similar moral conundrum to Chance and Dude, and *Rio Lobo* (1970) features Mitchum's son Christopher in the sidekick role as Duke updates the lead role a bit by portraying a Union officer out for justice after being attacked by Confederate raiders. But *Rio Bravo* remains the pair's best argument for their shared ideal vision of American justice. The characters in the film stand up to injustice because they know in their hearts it's the right thing to do, and their struggle reflects countless real-life examples from our country's history.

John Wayne, Constance
Towers and William Holden in
The Horse Soldiers (1959).

The Horse Soldiers

RELEASE 1959
DIRECTOR JOHN FORD

IN THIS Civil War film from John Ford, John Wayne's Colonel John Marlowe is sent on a mission to stealthily infiltrate Confederate territory. Frequently having to think fast when facing various dangers, Col. Marlowe differs from some of the enviable decision-makers Duke was known to play who seem to have all the answers despite the circumstances. When a group of military cadets starts opening fire all around him, the colonel isn't ashamed to tell the charming Hannah Hunter (Constance Towers) his plan: "With all due respect to your presence, ma'am, I'm gonna get the hell outta here." And when tensions between himself and Major Henry Kendall (William Holden) reach a boiling point prompting the men to head to the woods to settle the dispute, Marlowe takes a hit thanks to his decision to skip the parameters. "What are the rules gonna be, Colonel?" Kendall asks as the two prepare to fight. "Just make up your own!" Marlowe replies before receiving a swift fist to the jaw. But in true Duke fashion, Marlowe quickly gets back on his feet and drops Kendall with ease.

   With John Ford at the helm and John Wayne as the star, *The Horse Soldiers* had no trouble pleasing critics. *Saturday Review* praised the film's thrills, writing, "Its action scenes, as directed by the veteran John Ford, tingle with an excitement all too rare upon the screen these days."

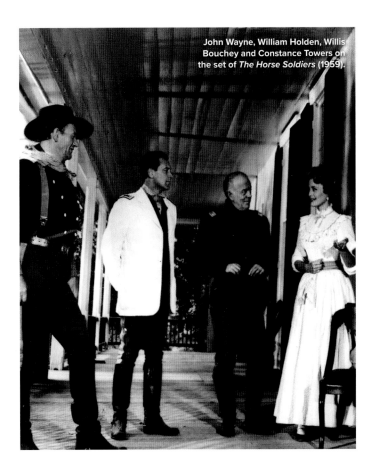

John Wayne, William Holden, Willis Bouchey and Constance Towers on the set of *The Horse Soldiers* (1959).

"You tangle with me, I'll have your hide."

—JOHN WAYNE AS COLONEL JOHN MARLOWE

★ ★ ★

John Wayne in *The Man Who Shot Liberty Valance* (1962).

CEMENTING HIS LEGACY

As he entered the 1960s, John Wayne was revered as an industry
veteran guaranteed to deliver classic after classic.

The Alamo

RELEASE 1960
DIRECTOR JOHN WAYNE

BY THE START of the 1950s, John Wayne had already been a mainstay in the movie industry for more than two decades. He worked his way up from the depths of B-movies and serials to the lofty peaks of A-list stardom, headlining classics such as *Back to Bataan* (1945), *Angel and the Badman* (1947) and *Red River* (1948), to name a few. Duke had accomplished more than most actors ever do, but the hardworking star wasn't one to simply rest on his laurels. As the smoke cleared from the battlefields of World War II and Americans slowly recovered from the horror of that conflict, John Wayne felt a calling to take his art to the next level in service of a generation that helped secure freedom at home and peace abroad. The biggest name in Hollywood would spend more than a decade trying to bring his dream, a film enshrining the ideals of this nation and the sacrifices sometimes required to preserve them, into cinematic reality. The result, 1960's *The Alamo*, "is an emotional reminder of what we respect— liberty, freedom and independence," says John Farkis, author of *Not Thinkin'...Just Rememberin'...The Making of John Wayne's The Alamo*, a comprehensive oral history of the Western epic he spent years researching and compiling. Today, the film's intent remains clear: It's a cinematic love letter from America's greatest actor to the country that gave him so much.

John Wayne never wavered in his belief that *The Alamo* was an important film America needed, but he had difficulty convincing the movie studios of the profitability of his vision. He first started seriously pursuing the idea with Republic Pictures in the late 1940s, and in 1947 he even scouted some filming locations near San Antonio. But Duke's insistence on directing and producing his passion project made potential backers nervous. "Though John Wayne was a fabulous actor and a box office money-maker, he was unknown as a director," Farkis says. "He thought he might just play a cameo in *The Alamo*, but the studios insisted he be one of the three major stars in the film." In 1956, John Wayne finally struck a deal with United Artists, which agreed to distribute and partially fund the prospective picture in exchange for Duke starring in *The Alamo* and three subsequent films. Combined with the investments made by individuals— including several Texan businessmen eager to have Duke at the helm of the Lone Star State's most-celebrated story—and John Wayne's own personal contribution, United Artists's backing gave the actor everything he needed to get started.

As difficult as it was for John Wayne to get the necessary funding, the true challenge had only begun. Duke didn't set out to make just another Western—he wanted to craft a film as epic and expansive

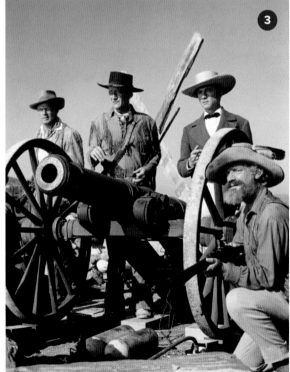

as his love for America. *The Alamo*'s budget would climb to $12 million before calling it a wrap, an astronomical figure in 1959. "Most films at the time had a budget of $3 to $5 million, maximum," Farkis says. "This was one of the most expensive films ever made up to that time." Part of the high costs stemmed from the army of actors, extras and the less glamorous—but very necessary—personnel Duke hired for the production. Around 340 people were part of the cast and crew, not to mention the 1,600 horses and the 45 members of the catering service needed to feed everyone. But John Wayne's most ambitious endeavor was the construction of the set, known as Alamo Village, in Brackettville, Texas. "It was a practical set, meaning that you could film inside the buildings. There were no false fronts," Farkis says. "This was a massive undertaking." The village, taking up 400 acres of Texas real estate, required more than one and a half million adobe bricks before its buildings were complete, including a to-scale replica of the Alamo Mission itself. Construction took two years between 1957 and '59, including a brief pause when Duke ran out of money and had to broker a deal with the land's owner, James Tullis "Happy" Shahan, to complete construction (Shahan acquired the right to lend out the village for other movies). But for John Wayne, creating his own movie set meant he wouldn't have to rent a studio soundstage and place himself at the mercy of another's schedule. "He could film whenever, wherever and however he wanted," Farkis says.

Duke paid a price for exerting so much control over *The Alamo*, and it wasn't always measured in dollars and cents. Taking on the roles of actor, director and producer increased the star's workload to titanic proportions, and he was forced into a constant balancing act between keeping down costs,

1. John Wayne, Richard Widmark and Laurence Harvey in *The Alamo* (1960). 2. Duke, unidentified and Chill Wills in a scene. 3. Richard Widmark, John Wayne, Laurence Harvey and John Dierkes in the film.

4. Duke directs *The Alamo*. 5. A jacket worn by John Wayne in the film. 6. A signed prop rifle used by Duke in *The Alamo*. 7. Duke and Richard Widmark in a scene.

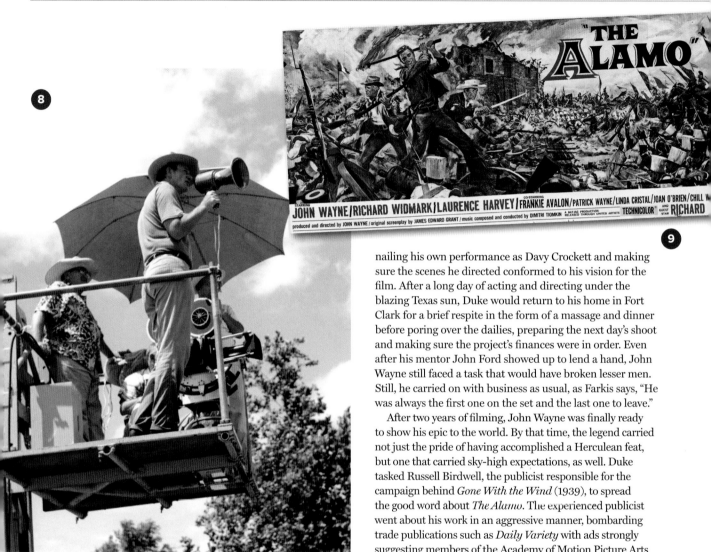

nailing his own performance as Davy Crockett and making sure the scenes he directed conformed to his vision for the film. After a long day of acting and directing under the blazing Texas sun, Duke would return to his home in Fort Clark for a brief respite in the form of a massage and dinner before poring over the dailies, preparing the next day's shoot and making sure the project's finances were in order. Even after his mentor John Ford showed up to lend a hand, John Wayne still faced a task that would have broken lesser men. Still, he carried on with business as usual, as Farkis says, "He was always the first one on the set and the last one to leave."

After two years of filming, John Wayne was finally ready to show his epic to the world. By that time, the legend carried not just the pride of having accomplished a Herculean feat, but one that carried sky-high expectations, as well. Duke tasked Russell Birdwell, the publicist responsible for the campaign behind *Gone With the Wind* (1939), to spread the good word about *The Alamo*. The experienced publicist went about his work in an aggressive manner, bombarding trade publications such as *Daily Variety* with ads strongly suggesting members of the Academy of Motion Picture Arts and Sciences who didn't cast a vote for *The Alamo* lacked a true love for the red, white and blue. "Once Wayne realized what Birdwell was doing, he told him to dial the campaign back a little," Farkis says. Of the seven Oscar nominations the film received, it won only an award for Best Sound. Audiences were kinder, however, and *The Alamo* managed to eventually

8. Duke directs *The Alamo*. **9.** A billboard poster for the film. **10.** John Wayne and Linda Cristal in a scene. **11.** Duke at the world premiere for *The Alamo*, which brought 20,000 people to the parking lot of a Handy Andy grocery store.

break even. Duke himself didn't make a dime from the film, but he still counted himself richer for the experience of creating it. What sustained John Wayne through the movie's hellish shooting schedule wasn't the dream of adding zeros to his bank account or picking up an Oscar—it was making a fitting tribute to the American values of freedom and sacrifice. "He wanted to send that message out to the world," Farkis says, "and it comes through loud and clear."

"Ya don't get lard less'n you boil a hog!"

—JOHN WAYNE AS DAVY CROCKETT

Duke, Stewart Granger and Capucine in *North to Alaska* (1960).

North to Alaska

RELEASE 1960
DIRECTOR HENRY HATHAWAY

IN THE ALASKAN city of Nome, John Wayne's Sam McCord and his mining partner George Pratt (Stewart Granger) have struck gold. As George puts the finishing touches on the honeymoon cabin he's been building for his fiancée Jenny (Lilyan Chauvin), McCord travels to Seattle to bring his partner's bride-to-be to Nome—only to find that she's moved on and married another man. Wondering how he'll break the news, McCord hires "Angel" aka Michelle (Capucine), a prostitute, to ease the pain a little. But though Michelle is brought to Alaska to help heal George's heartbreak, she quickly develops feelings for the emotionally closed-off McCord, who avoids every opportunity to reciprocate affection. Finally, when the woman is about to leave town for good, the macho miner decides it's time to put it all on the line and tell Michelle how he feels.

Thanks to its balance of humor and heart, *North to Alaska* won over the critics. *Variety* called it "the sort of easy-going, slap-happy entertainment that doesn't come around so often anymore in films," adding, "Wayne displays a genuine flair for the lighthearted approach." Soon after, *The New York Times* dubbed the film "pleasantly boisterous," crediting the charismatic star with driving it to success, stating, "the proceedings are easily dominated by the indefatigable Mr. Wayne."

John Wayne in a wardrobe test shot for *North to Alaska* (1960).

"*George, a wonderful thing about Alaska is that matrimony hasn't hit up here yet. Let's keep it a free country!*"

—JOHN WAYNE AS SAM MCCORD

★ ★ ★

The Comancheros

RELEASE 1961
DIRECTOR MICHAEL CURTIZ, JOHN WAYNE (UNCREDITED)

AT THE TIME OF the release of *The Comancheros* on October 30, 1961, John Wayne was at yet another turning point in his career. One year prior, the star brought a passion project to life when he starred in and directed *The Alamo*, proving definitively that his prowess was not restricted to one side of the camera. And though Duke would initially only sign on to star in *The Comancheros*, unfortunate circumstances during production of the Western would yield another opportunity for the actor to take the reins as director.

Shot in Moab, Utah, in the summer of 1961, the film would be helmed by prolific filmmaker Michael Curtiz, who had already achieved legendary status for his work on the 1942 classic *Casablanca*. *The Comancheros* was a reunion of sorts for the actor and the director, with Duke having worked as an extra in Curtiz's 1928 film *Noah's Ark* before starring in his 1953 comedy-drama *Trouble Along the Way*. But the chance to craft a classic Western together would also end up being the last time the two industry titans would collaborate. Throughout production, Curtiz was entrenched in a battle with cancer that often left him unable to make it to the set. Eventually, Duke offered to step in and helm the remainder of the film to ensure Curtiz's vision would not go unrealized.

While he may not have been expecting to jump into the director's chair, John Wayne was plenty prepared for the task. As authentically Western as the red rock canyons surrounding the city in which it was shot, *The Comancheros* is a shining example of Duke's ability to push a story to its greatest, most entertaining potential. The legend stars as Captain Jake Cutter, a Texas Ranger who arrests Paul Regret (Stuart Whitman), a notorious gambler and possible murderer. When the two encounter a violent gang of outlaws known as the Comancheros, however, they find themselves with no choice but to join forces in an effort to survive. While not always the safest creative choice for a Western, the adversaries-turned-allies story is exactly the type of bold territory John Wayne could navigate with ease.

In addition to his recent directorial experience and his decades of playing an outlaw-toppling cowboy, Duke had the comfort of

familiar faces on the set of *The Comancheros*. The film would provide an overdue reunion between John Wayne and actor Bruce Cabot, who plays Major Henry. Friends from their time together in *Angel and the Badman* (1947), the two actors had not worked alongside each other in 14 years until *The Comancheros* brought them back together on screen. Also joining Duke in the cast was his own son, Patrick Wayne, who plays Tobe, a young Texas ranger who teams up with Jake and Regret in the quest to stop the outlaws. Having appeared in films including *The Searchers* (1956) and *The Alamo* (1960), John Wayne's second son already had respectable experience to speak of by the time he stepped onto the set of *The Comancheros*. But that didn't mean his time under Duke's learning tree was complete. When it became apparent he didn't look quite as

natural saddling up on a horse as his famous father did, the younger Wayne found himself on the receiving end of some tough love. "The dailies came back and they looked awful," Patrick recalls. "My father said, 'You're going to learn how to ride now or get out of the business.'"

Fortunately, Patrick did indeed learn to ride, and *The Comancheros* was anything but awful in the eyes of audiences and critics. *Variety* labeled the film "a big, brash, uninhibited action-western of the old school, about as subtle as a right to the jaw." In 1962, *The Comancheros* would go on to win the Bronze Wrangler Award from the Western Heritage Center

1. John Wayne in *The Comancheros* (1961).
2. John Wayne, Bruce Cabot and Guinn "Big Boy" Williams in a scene from the film.

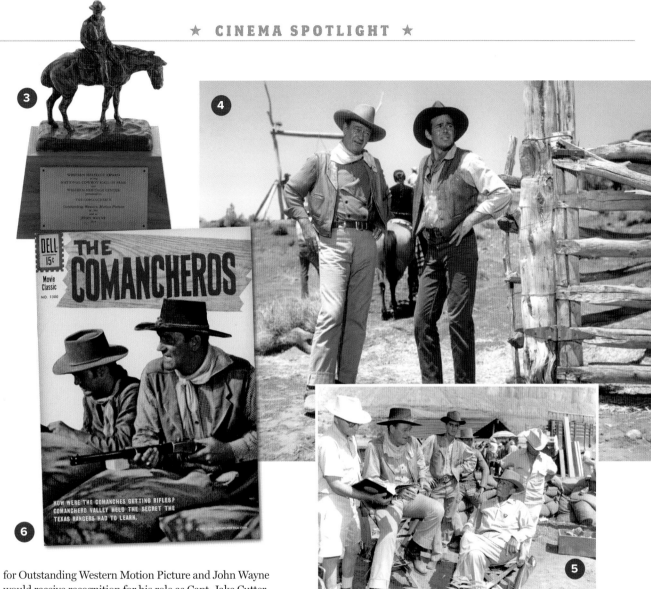

for Outstanding Western Motion Picture and John Wayne would receive recognition for his role as Capt. Jake Cutter when he received the Golden Laurel Award for Top Action Performance. Sadly, Michael Curtiz would not see the film's success, as he passed away shortly before its release. John Wayne would pay his respects through humility—despite his own efforts behind the camera, he insisted Curtiz be the only credited director on the film.

3. A trophy from The National Cowboy Hall of Fame and Western Heritage Center for Outstanding Western Motion Picture. **4.** Duke and Stuart Whitman in *The Comancheros*. **5.** Duke and Michael Curtiz on set. **6.** *The Comancheros* Dell comic book.

The Man Who Shot Liberty Valance

RELEASE 1962
DIRECTOR JOHN FORD

THE CHARACTERS JOHN Wayne played over the course of his 50-year career are no strangers to suffering. On multiple occasions, the actor played men who were beaten, bludgeoned, shot and left for dead by the various nefarious men they encountered. But only one of Duke's characters completely lost everything that truly mattered to him: Tom Doniphon in John Ford's melancholic *The Man Who Shot Liberty Valance* (1962). Ford always excelled at guiding his protégé into new and exciting roles, from the fearless Ringo Kid in *Stagecoach* (1939) to the fearsome Ethan Edwards in *The Searchers* (1956). With *The Man Who Shot Liberty Valance*, the masterful director took Duke in a bold new direction by having the actor showcase all of the attributes that made him beloved to audiences—his authenticity, his vitality, his charisma—and subverting them completely by revealing their futility against staving off the future.

The film's plot follows James Stewart's Ransom Stoddard, a successful politician, as he arrives in the town of Shinbone and recounts how years earlier he helped free the community from the tyrannical grip of the violent outlaw Liberty Valance (Lee Marvin). Doniphon aids the tender-footed lawyer in his struggle against Valance, but the two protagonists clash over philosophy—Doniphon lives by the way of the gun, in opposition to Stoddard's devotion to rule of law—and over a woman named Hallie (Vera Miles). In the climactic showdown between Stoddard and Valance, Doniphon secretly takes out the villain himself by shooting from the shadows, but allows Stoddard to claim the credit. He also lets the lawyer win the heart of Hallie, realizing the age of the gunslinger has ended and the West now belongs to booksmart men such as Stoddard. Stewart's character goes on to find success as a politician, while Doniphon dies alone in obscurity. The respective fates of the film's two leads isn't the result of choices made by either man, but presented by Ford as the simple, unstoppable course of history.

The theme of time's irresistible pull must have held a special attraction for the 67-year-old Ford, who had been making movies since the silent film era. It's disputed whether the decision to shoot the movie in black and white and on a studio set came from Ford, or whether Paramount forced it upon the director in order to limit costs. But the resulting photography sets the mood for the movie, announcing with its stark visuals that this Western will focus more on contrasting characters and how they react to the inevitabilities in life rather than the romantic, sweeping vistas of Monument Valley.

Audiences didn't seem deterred by the shift in tone, turning out in droves to see *The Man Who Shot Liberty Valance*. The film earned an estimated $8 million at the box office from a $3.2 million budget, making it one of 1962's most financially successful films. The Western also succeeded critically. A review from *The New York Times* reads, "The mayhem, murder and downright colorful cussedness inspired by the seemingly indestructible struggle between

1. John Wayne on the set of *The Man Who Shot Liberty Valance* (1962). **2.** A one sheet for the film. **3.** John Wayne and Vera Miles in a scene. **4.** Lee Van Cleef, Lee Marvin, James Stewart and John Wayne in the Western.

cattlemen and homesteaders is handled with consummate professionalism by such top hands as John Ford, director; James Stewart and John Wayne."

Tom Doniphon's tragic end may run counter to most of the cowboys John Wayne brought to life on-screen, but the role captures a truth fundamental to the actor's appeal: You can't choose what life throws at you, but you can choose how to react to it. Doniphon accepted his fate with honor and dignity, caring for the ones he loved. Nobody would expect anything less of a character played by John Wayne.

5. James Stewart, Woody Strode and Duke in *The Man Who Shot Liberty Valance*. **6.** A Stetson cowboy hat worn by John Wayne in the film. **7.** A bib-style shirt worn by John Wayne in the Western and also featured in the artwork for the film's poster. **8.** Duke in the film.

John Wayne says "pilgrim" a total of 23 times in the film.

8

Hatari!

RELEASE 1962
DIRECTOR HOWARD HAWKS

JOHN WAYNE KNEW he could always succeed by donning a ten-gallon hat and wielding a six-shooter on the big screen, but the legend also liked a challenge. In the early 1960s, Duke was given an opportunity to stray far from his Western roots by starring in *Hatari!* (1962), a safari film that would see the legend as Sean Mercer, a big game catcher exploring Africa and falling in love along the way. Much like his character, by taking the job, John Wayne was embarking on an adventure he would not forget.

With director Howard Hawks at the helm of *Hatari!*, Duke knew the unlikely role was in very capable hands. The two first worked together on the 1948 classic *Red River*, in which Hawks took the actor out of his comfort zone by having him play a true villain in the dastardly Tom Dunson. When they worked together a second time for *Rio Bravo* in 1959, Hawks returned John Wayne to familiar form as the moral, no-nonsense sheriff John T. Chance. Both films were widely revered and benefited from an undeniable creative chemistry between Hawks and Duke, while *Hatari!* gave the pair the chance to take their collaboration into truly uncharted territory.

As principal photography began for the film in November 1960, John Wayne traveled to Tanganyika, East Africa, a first-time shooting location for the legend. Upon arriving at the production's base camp—which was located about 60 miles west of Mount Kilimanjaro on the edge of the Serengeti—some of Duke's less experienced castmates became flustered and anxious when they learned copies of the shooting script didn't make the trip. Having worked with Hawks and other directors of his style before, John Wayne was able to quell the concerns. "The greatest directors, including Hawks, never handed me a script," the legend told one of his biographers. "You just have to

trust them. If you're good, they'll show you to your best advantage day by day." In fact, Duke trusted Hawks's production so much that when it came to working with the wild animals, the star opted to do most of the dangerous scenes himself rather than relying on a double. But the authentic African setting proved to be unpredictable as John Wayne encountered some of the wildlife while he was off the clock. One night after a day of shooting, Duke and his costar Red Buttons were playing a game of cards outside their tents when a wild leopard emerged from the shadows and came creeping toward them. Completely at ease with the situation, Duke simply quipped to his pal, "Buttons, see what he wants."

The comedic chemistry John Wayne and Red Buttons shared between takes translates perfectly within the action of *Hatari!* But while Buttons's character Pockets provides many of the film's most humorous moments, Duke's Sean Mercer makes *Hatari!* a more tender offering than some may expect from an African adventure film. Amid the danger of trying to catch everything from rhinos to zebras, Mercer falls for Elsa Martinelli's character Dallas, a photographer aiming to capture the wildlife on film rather than in cages. Of course, Mercer tries to put business first and suppress his true feelings as long as possible. Once it appears Dallas might become the one who got away, though, the big game catcher follows his heart and employs baby elephants to help him track her down. When Mercer finds Dallas, he proposes as the exotic mammals look on. Duke would even compliment the acting skills of one

1. Elsa Martinelli and John Wayne in *Hatari!* (1962). **2.** Duke and Red Buttons (born Aaron Chwatt) chat between takes on the set of the film.

3. Duke and Hardy Krüger with a giraffe on set.
4. A *Hatari!* six sheet.
5. Duke and Hardy Krüger with a secretary bird on set. 6. Duke with a cheetah between takes.
7. A custom *Hatari!* mug.

8. John Wayne, cinematographer Russell Harlan and Howard Hawks on location for *Hatari!* 9. Duke in action in a scene from the film. 10. Hardy Krüger, John Wayne, Red Buttons and Michéle Girardon in a scene. 11. Hardy Krüger, John Wayne and other cast members ride, with their vehicles, on a raft in a river on the set of *Hatari!*

of the baby elephants while shooting the film's final scene, instead blaming the need for numerous takes on himself. As Mercer and Dallas are celebrating their romantic promise, an elephant gets onto the bed and sends it crashing down. After about 18 attempts at the scene, Duke conceded, "He's doing it right, I'm not."

Fortunately, the adventurous role paid off as many critics who saw him in *Hatari!* felt John Wayne was "doing it right." *Variety*'s review stated the star "plays with his customary effortless (or so it seems) authority a role which he identified." Giving the film perhaps its highest praise was Peter Bogdanovich, who wrote in *Film Culture*, "Without question, *Hatari!* is among the best American pictures of 1962," even going as far as to say, "Anyone who does not see the beauty and brilliance of this film is either a fool or a snob, and both are really the same."

From left: Steve Forrest, John Wayne, Tom Tryon and Stuart Whitman in *The Longest Day* (1962).

The Longest Day

RELEASE 1962
DIRECTORS KEN ANNAKIN, ANDREW MARTON, BERNHARD WICKI

USING CORNELIUS RYAN'S book *The Longest Day* as inspiration, this historical film features John Wayne as Lieutenant Colonel Benjamin Vandervoort, the D-Day hero who fought through a German counterattack with a broken leg after parachuting into France. On full display are pivotal moments such as General Eisenhower facing the decision to launch the Normandy invasion, acted out by Henry Grace with palpable tension. The perspective of the other side is given screen time, too, as scenes of the increasingly distressed German forces are parsed through the film. And then there is, of course, John Wayne's Vandervoort to provide one of the most shining examples of heroism contained in the story, hobbling on one leg to continue fighting to the bitter end.

Combining the cohesive vision created by its team of directors, the lingering weight of the film's true events and the reliable realism displayed in Duke's performance, *The Longest Day* enlightened audiences to the events of D-Day unlike anything that had come before it. The film earned resounding acclaim, including a *New York Times* review that concluded, "It is hard to think of a picture, aimed and constructed as this one was, doing any more or any better or leaving one feeling any more exposed to the horror of war than this one does."

John Wayne and
Harry Morgan in
*How the West Was
Won* (1962)

How the West Was Won

RELEASE 1962
DIRECTORS JOHN FORD,
HENRY HATHAWAY, GEORGE MARSHALL

WITH TWO OF his greatest collaborators John Ford and Henry Hathaway at the helm, Duke was destined to make the most of his minimal screen time as General William Tecumseh Sherman in this sprawling story of the settlers who dared to claim the sea of wilderness that became the American West. As for the cast, John Wayne was joined by fellow Hollywood heavy hitters of the era including James Stewart as Linus Rawlings, Gregory Peck as Cleve Van Valen and Henry Fonda as Jethro Stuart. In a pivotal scene with Harry Morgan, who plays then-General Ulysses S. Grant, John Wayne's presence is particularly powerful. When the newspapers criticize his handling of the Battle of Shiloh, Gen. Grant tells Gen. Sherman, "Win or lose tomorrow, I intend to resign." With all the gusto one would expect of a John Wayne character, fictional or not, Sherman insists Grant disregard what anyone else thinks and just follow his heart.

How the West Was Won had no trouble winning over critics. The April 1963 edition of *Christian Science Monitor* called the film "A monumental effort that achieves monumental success," while *Photoplay* simply named it "Best picture of the year."

"It doesn't matter what the people think, it's what you think."

—JOHN WAYNE AS GENERAL WILLIAM TECUMSEH SHERMAN

Donovan's Reef

RELEASE 1963
DIRECTOR **JOHN FORD**

The film's working title was *The Climate of Love.*

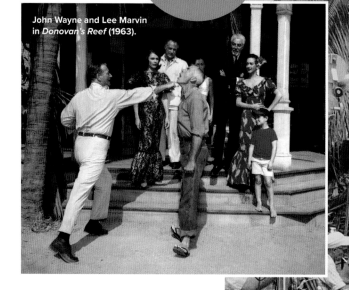

John Wayne and Lee Marvin in *Donovan's Reef* (1963).

IN THEIR FINAL film together, Duke and John Ford managed to make a perfect tribute to the type of after-hours mischief that marked their friendship over the years. *Donovan's Reef* (1963) sees John Wayne as Michael Patrick "Guns" Donovan, a World War II hero spending his civilian life as the owner of Donovan's Reef, a saloon on the tranquil Polynesian island of Haleakaloha. Each year on December 7, however, Donovan and his war buddy Aloysius "Boats" Gilhooley (Lee Marvin) disturb the peace by engaging in an unorthodox holiday tradition: an anything-goes friendly bar brawl that sees the two punching each other onto pianos, slamming each other through tables and throwing anything but the bottle of brandy (seemingly Donovan's only rule). In addition to the slapstick fighting—which was inspired by Duke's real-life exhibition scraps with his buddy Ward Bond—the film's comedy comes from the personality clash between Donovan and Amelia Dedham (Elizabeth Allen), the estranged daughter of his other war buddy, Doc Dedham (Jack Warden). Arriving on the island in hopes of overtaking the family shipping line, the city slicker Amelia threatens the carefree vibe Donovan has established on the island—but that doesn't stop him from having fun at her expense. When Donovan begrudgingly takes Amelia waterskiing, she shows off by egging him on to drive the boat faster, to which he gleefully obliges until she crashes face-first into the water.

Recognizing Duke and Ford's intent to make something reflective of their laugh-filled friendship for their final outing, *The New York Herald Tribune* praised the film's "good, clean, simple-minded fun." After making plenty of masterpieces, the legendary duo just wanted to make 'em laugh.

John Ford and John Wayne on the set of *Donovan's Reef* (1963).

McLintock!

RELEASE 1963
DIRECTOR ANDREW V. MCLAGLEN

THE FIRST OF several collaborations between John Wayne and director Andrew V. McLaglen, 1963's *McLintock!* sees Duke as rich rancher George Washington "G.W." McLintock, who has his hands full between the farmers, government workers, Native Americans and fellow ranchers all fighting over local land. McLintock also has major issues with his estranged wife Katherine (Maureen O'Hara), whom he often deals with in public to the delight of the onlooking townspeople. Eventually, all of McLintock's dirty laundry comes together: When an incident boils over between the rancher and a shotgun-wielding man, McLintock gives the troublemaker a stern warning before abruptly changing his mind and socking him in the jaw, sending him barreling down the hill into a mud pond. This causes the surrounding onlookers—including Katherine McLintock—to erupt into an all-out brawl, slinging literal mud in a scene that's as cathartic as it is hilarious.

Critics commended Duke's ability to deliver a fresh, funny take on the Western genre that he had spent decades of his career perfecting with the utmost seriousness. *Variety* wrote, "Wayne is about the last thriving exponent of a great tradition, the last active member of a select fraternity of larger-than-life Western film heroes."

"Pilgrim, you caused a lot of trouble this morning, might have got somebody killed...and somebody oughta belt you in the mouth. But I won't, I won't, the hell I won't!"

—JOHN WAYNE AS G.W. MCLINTOCK

John Wayne, Maureen O'Hara and Edgar Buchanan in *McLintock!* (1963). Opposite: Big John Hamilton, Duke and Patrick Wayne in the film.

Circus World

RELEASE 1964
DIRECTOR HENRY HATHAWAY

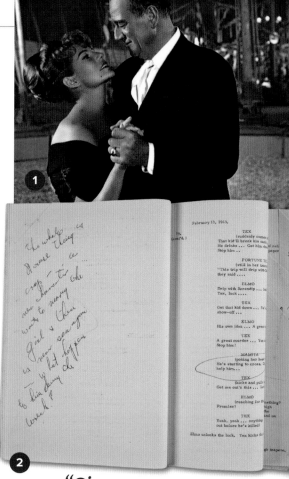

EVEN AFTER MORE than three decades on the silver screen, John Wayne wanted to continue taking the occasional risk that would remind moviegoers just how versatile he could be. With his final film with mentor John Ford behind him, the legend entered a new defining phase of collaboration as he began a run of films with Henry Hathaway, a director he had previously only worked with about once per decade. Much like *Legend of the Lost* (1957) before it, *Circus World* (1964) was enthralling evidence of the bold mastery the filmmaker and star were capable of together.

Hathaway's productions often took John Wayne to locales far from America, and *Circus World* was no different. In September of 1963, the legend boarded a plane to Barcelona, Spain, where he would work on the Western-adjacent drama for nearly half a year. Beyond the thrill of shooting in the picturesque European city, Duke would also get to star alongside a fellow Hollywood icon, Rita Hayworth. *Circus World* marks the only occasion in which the two stars worked together, and the exclusivity of their obvious chemistry makes the film all the better.

After taking his show to Europe, John Wayne's circus proprietor Matt Masters is determined to track down his long-lost lover Lili Alfredo (Rita Hayworth), the mother of the girl he has raised as his own daughter, Toni (Claudia Cardinale). As his circus and Wild West Shows gain success across the continent, Masters remains focused on finding Lili. When the two finally reunite in an embrace at one of the show's final performances, viewers are treated to one of the better romantic scenes of Duke's later years. After Lili confesses, "God help me, but I still love you, Matt," Masters brings the pair's relationship full circle, telling her, "That's nothing to be ashamed of, then or now."

Following the release of *Circus World*, critics took note of Henry Hathaway's skill for bringing out the best in John Wayne. *Variety* wrote, "Of Wayne it may be said that he is the center pole, the muscle, the virility and the incarnate courage of this often down but never out circus. The role has been tailored to his talents and personality." Like a trapeze artist, John Wayne always knew how to wow a crowd with his skillful flexibility.

"Give me your knife—I'm not gonna lose another damn tent!"

—DUKE AS MATT MASTERS
(SAVING A TENT FROM A FIRE)

★ ★ ★

1. Rita Hayworth and John Wayne in *Circus World* (1964). **2.** Duke's annotated script for the film. **3.** John Wayne in the film.

John Wayne in
Circus World (1964).

John Wayne in
*The Greatest Story
Ever Told* (1965).

In Harm's Way
shot aboard
several U.S. Navy
ships, including the
U.S.S. Braine and
U.S.S. Walker.

The Greatest Story Ever Told

RELEASE 1965
DIRECTORS GEORGE STEVENS, DAVID LEAN,
JEAN NEGULESCO

THOUGH JOHN WAYNE was a star of biblical proportions by 1965, few could have predicted that he would have a role in a film about the life and teachings of Jesus Christ. Prior to *The Greatest Story Ever Told*, Duke's only experience in a big screen Bible-inspired story was in Michael Curtiz's *Noah's Ark* in 1928, in which he and Ward Bond worked as extras in a flood scene. This time, however, the Western icon would take on a more notable role, playing a centurion at the Crucifixion who utters perhaps the film's most famous line.

"Truly, this man was the Son of God."

—JOHN WAYNE AS CENTURION AT CRUCIFIXION

★ ★ ★

In Harm's Way

RELEASE 1965
DIRECTOR OTTO PREMINGER

FOLLOWING THE ATTACKS on Pearl Harbor, John Wayne's Captain Rockwell "Rock" Torrey is tasked with leading his crew in a cat-and-mouse chase seeking retaliation against the Japanese forces. When he discovers an essential crew member, Commander Paul Eddington (Kirk Douglas), is struggling to set aside problems with his wife and focus on the mission, Capt. Torrey does his best to be understanding while also helping Eddington snap out of the distraction. Eventually, as further attacks loom, Capt. Torrey is joined on deck by a refreshed Comdr. Eddington—just in time to prepare for the massive battle that marks the film's dramatic climax.

Kirk Douglas and John Wayne in *In Harm's Way* (1965).

The Sons of Katie Elder

RELEASE 1965
DIRECTOR HENRY HATHAWAY

BY THE TIME he arrived in Mexico to begin shooting *The Sons of Katie Elder* in January 1965, John Wayne was enjoying one of the greatest eras of his career. With decades of experience under his belt at this point, the actor was already a certified cinema legend—and he had plenty of stellar performances left in the tank. But between the possibility of having to relinquish his role and the nature of the film's story, *The Sons of Katie Elder* would be just as personally significant for Duke as it was professionally.

Production for the film was initially slated for October 1964, but when John Wayne's bout with cancer forced him to be in a hospital bed rather than on a movie set, the process was put on hold. While never one to throw in the towel, Duke was pragmatic about the situation. As he recovered from having half of his left lung removed, the star suggested to producer Hal B. Wallis and director Henry Hathaway that Kirk Douglas replace him in the role in order to keep the film on track. But Hathaway, who first worked with Duke more than two decades prior on *The Shepherd of the Hills* (1941), knew from first-hand experience that—all due respect to Kirk Douglas—John Wayne was irreplaceable. And having won

his own battle with colon cancer that same year, the director was more than understanding and told Duke to come to work once he was on the mend. In a move that shouldn't surprise anyone who knew him well, just two months later, John Wayne showed up for work. As the gruff gunslinger John Elder, the star was right back in action as if he hadn't just had major surgery for a life-threatening illness. And knowing Duke was up to the task, Hathaway didn't water down the physicality the role called for. "Well, old Henry was very thoughtful of me, of course, since I was recuperating and all," John Wayne joked to Roger Ebert in a 1968 interview. "He took me up to 8,500 feet to shoot the damned thing, and the fourth day of shooting he had me jumping into ice water. Very considerate."

In addition to Hathaway, Dean Martin was another familiar face John Wayne got to see on set. Duke had first joined forces with the singing superstar and variety TV sensation in 1959's *Rio Bravo*, one of the most beloved films of either man's career. And much like it was a reunion for Duke with Martin and Hathaway, *The Sons of Katie Elder* centers on the reuniting of John Elder and his brothers Tom (Dean Martin), Matt (Earl Holliman) and Bud (Michael Anderson Jr.) in Clearwater, Texas, for

their revered mother's funeral. As the two eldest Elder brothers, John and Tom lead their younger siblings in a mission to uncover the truth about their father's death while also dealing with the loss of their mother. When the entrepreneur Morgan Hastings (James Gregory) suspiciously claims to have won the family ranch in a poker game just prior to the Elder patriarch being shot and killed, it becomes all but certain who the brothers must extract vengeance from. Eventually, the climactic confirmation of Hastings's villainous deed comes from the mouth of his own son Dave, played by Dennis Hopper just a few years prior to his major breakout role in *Easy Rider* (1969). The scene is just as important to the plot as it is to cinema as a whole—the sight of Duke's John Elder listening to the vindicating words of Hopper's character would be the first time the two Hollywood legends shared the screen. Long after John Wayne's passing, Hopper continued to praise the icon, telling *InContention.com* in 2008, "He was a hell of a finer actor than he was given credit for being while he was alive."

While his acting prowess may have been underappreciated by some at the time, John Wayne did receive hearty praise from critics for his performance in the film. The actor's signature stamp on Western cinema was well established by the mid-1960s, as *Variety* wrote, "Wayne delivers one of his customary rugged portrayals," while *The New York Daily News* considered him an essential element to the genre: "[It] has what

---

1. John Wayne, Dean Martin, Earl Holliman and Michael Anderson Jr. in *The Sons of Katie Elder* (1965). **2.** Duke and Martha Hyer in the film. **3.** Duke and Dean Martin put their footprints in cement at the Campo Mexico Hotel. **4.** A six sheet for the film.

every bang-up Western ought to have, an unaffected story, striking scenery and John Wayne."

And beyond Duke's impressive performance, *The Sons of Katie Elder* continues to resonate thanks to its universal themes. As the brothers quickly discover in the film, trying times are sure to make the bonds of family stronger than ever. That lesson, like John Wayne himself, will always be relevant.

5. Duke and Dean Martin in *The Sons of Katie Elder*. **6.** John Wayne in the film. **7.** John Wayne, Dean Martin and Earl Holliman carry Michael Anderson Jr. in a scene from the film. **8.** John Wayne and Dennis Hopper in *The Sons of Katie Elder*.

John Wayne
and Dean Martin in
*The Sons of Katie
Elder* (1965).

John Wayne and Kirk Douglas in *Cast a Giant Shadow* (1966).

"Give this insubordinate son-of-a-bitch every truck and every blanket in the Third Army. And I don't care who you have to steal them from!"

—JOHN WAYNE AS GENERAL MIKE RANDOLPH

Cast a Giant Shadow

RELEASE 1966
DIRECTOR MELVILLE SHAVELSON

JUST ONE YEAR after lighting up the screen with Kirk Douglas in *In Harm's Way* (1965), John Wayne would display his chemistry with his fellow cinema legend-in-the-making again in this historical drama from director Melville Shavelson. This time, the duo would dive deeper into the lasting horrors of World War II, providing audiences with a rare moment of vulnerability from the famously tough Duke. As Douglas's D-Day veteran Colonel David "Mickey" Marcus details the suffering of his people in the Holocaust—from the average weight of survivors being 85 pounds to the ovens that "no one ever baked any bread in"—John Wayne's General Mike Randolph quietly listens as his expression becomes increasingly distressed. Once Col. Marcus reveals that the concentration camp contains roughly 3,200 unburied corpses, Gen. Randolph is overcome as he walks over to a fence and buries his face in his arm.

The haunting reminder of the conflict, shown through Duke's powerful performance, would leave quite an impression on viewers for years to come. In Lee Pfeiffer's 1989 book *The John Wayne Scrapbook*, the author writes, "Although Wayne appeared only for 11 minutes throughout the film, his services are quite memorable and well-acted."

Robert Mitchum, Arthur Hunnicutt and John Wayne in *El Dorado* (1966).

> *"Next time you shoot somebody, don't go near 'em 'til you're sure they're dead!"*

—JOHN WAYNE AS COLE THORNTON

★ ★ ★

El Dorado

RELEASE 1966
DIRECTOR HOWARD HAWKS

IN THIS ACTION-PACKED Western from Howard Hawks, one of the finest directors Duke would ever work with, John Wayne plays Cole Thornton, a rugged gunslinger who heads to the film's titular town to help rancher Bart Jason wage war against the McDonald family. But once Thornton gets word that the job might force him to fight against his old friend Sheriff J.P. Harrah (Robert Mitchum), he backs out. Months later, after learning Jason has hired a replacement gunman named Nelse McLeod (Christopher George) and Sheriff Harrah has developed a drinking problem, Thornton returns to El Dorado. Joined by the inexperienced youngster Mississippi (James Caan), Thornton wields his shotgun with fury and expertise as he helps the McDonald family defend their ranch against Jason and his dangerous crew.

El Dorado reminded critics that, even after so many years of hard work, John Wayne and Howard Hawks were still firing on all cylinders. *Variety* praised all aspects of the film, calling it "an excellent oater drama filled with adroit comedy and action relief and set off by strong casting, superior direction and solid production."

John Wayne and Robert Mitchum in *El Dorado* (1966).

To promote
The War Wagon, Duke
appeared as himself on the
November 21, 1966, episode
of *The Lucy Show*, meeting
the hijinks-prone star
after she spills ketchup
on his lap in a
restaurant.

The War Wagon

RELEASE 1967
DIRECTOR BURT KENNEDY

AFTER A PAIR of winning performances in two solemn films focusing on events from World War II, 1965's *In Harm's Way* and 1966's *Cast a Giant Shadow*, John Wayne and Kirk Douglas were given the chance to bring their big screen chemistry to a rip-roaring Western with *The War Wagon* (1967). With the common goal of stealing gold from a nefarious miner, Duke's Jackson and Douglas's Lomax team up to take down their common enemy. Trouble naturally follows them along the way, but the pair prove to be more than just tough-talking cowboys—they're also some of the quickest gunmen around. When a couple of outlaws attempt a sneak attack, Jackson and Lomax simultaneously spin around and shoot down their foolish foes in one fell swoop. "Mine hit the ground first," says Lomax. "Mine was taller," quips Jackson.

   Duke and Douglas were known to be chops-busting pals behind the scenes, and *The War Wagon* put that natural repartee on full display. *Variety* called the film "an entertaining, exciting Western drama of revenge, laced with action and humor," while *Time* wrote, "Wayne at 60 and Douglas at 50 can still invest any screenplay with style and gusto."

Kirk Douglas and John Wayne in *The War Wagon* (1967).

The Green Berets

RELEASE 1968
DIRECTOR JOHN WAYNE

I N THE LATE 1960s, most of Hollywood was not yet ready to make movies about the hot-button subject of Vietnam. John Wayne, however, was more than willing to lead the charge, choosing to see through the partisanship and get right to the heart of the matter: these were brave, young Americans risking life and limb in a far off land, unsure when—or if—they would return home. Initially inspired by Robin Moore's 1965 book *The Green Berets*, which details the author's experiences with Special Forces in Vietnam, the star felt the call of duty telling him to make a film about the courageous men facing unthinkable hell on the other side of the world. Under the banner of his production company Batjac, John Wayne set out to direct and star in what would become *The Green Berets* (1968).

Prior to production, Duke decided to go straight to the top in his quest to gain the resources necessary for the film. On December 28, 1965, the star penned a letter to President Lyndon B. Johnson addressing the polarizing nature of the war in Vietnam, writing, "Though I personally support the Administration's policy there, I know it is not a popular war, and I think it is extremely important that not only the people of the United States but people all over the world should know why it is necessary for us to be there." John Wayne's proposed solution, of course, was to make a rousing film about the American heroes serving in the conflict. "We want to tell the story of our fighting men in Vietnam with reason, emotion, characterization and action," Duke told President Johnson. "We want to do it in a manner that will inspire a patriotic attitude on the part of fellow Americans—a feeling which we have always had in this country in the past during times of stress and trouble."

The legend's request was granted, and he would soon begin work on *The Green Berets* with the cooperation of the United States Department of Defense. The Army post at Fort Benning, Georgia, would provide the setting for most of the film's exterior

"Out here, due process is a bullet!"

—JOHN WAYNE AS COLONEL MIKE KIRBY

1

scenes, including the climactic Battle of Nam Dang. Personnel, props and other bases were also made available to the production by the Pentagon, and Duke spared no expense when it came to ensuring the film's realism, digging deep into the Batjac budget whenever additional details were needed.

Beyond filling the set with authentic U.S. military equipment, John Wayne was also able to inject the actual perspective of those in Vietnam into the film. As he had previously done during World War II, the legend teamed up with the USO's Hollywood Overseas Committee and the U.S. Department of Defense to set out on a tour to Southeast Asia in the summer of 1966. Much more than a research opportunity for *The Green Berets*, John Wayne's visit "gave the kids something else to write home about," as he put it in an interview with *Stars and Stripes*.

Invigorated by his experience meeting the troops in

1. Jim Hutton, John Wayne, Aldo Ray and Raymond St. Jacques on the set of *The Green Berets* (1968). **2.** Duke and Edward Faulkner on the set of the film **3.** The beret worn by Duke in the film. **4.** A one sheet for *The Green Berets*. **5.** Duke in the film.

5

6

Vietnam, Duke donned the green beret with patriotic pride to play the hard-nosed Colonel Mike Kirby. As is the case with any of the films in which he plays a member of the Armed Forces, John Wayne's performance in *The Green Berets* beams with all the strength, conviction and never-say-die spirit one would expect to find in a real-life war hero. The critics, however, were largely unkind to the film as many couldn't help but focus on the film's perceived politics rather than the performance and production. But, ultimately, it didn't matter—as far as Duke was concerned, he had accomplished his mission. Much like Kirby's line to the young war orphan Hamchunk at the end of the film, *The Green Berets* was John Wayne's way of telling the troops, "You're what this is all about."

6. Raymond St. Jacques, John Wayne and George Takei in *The Green Berets*. **7.** Duke in the film.
8. John Wayne's annotated script for the film.
9. David Janssen, John Wayne and Craig Jue on the set of the film.

Hellfighters

RELEASE 1968
DIRECTOR ANDREW V. MCLAGLEN

I N THE LATE 1960s, just before he entered the final decade of his career, John Wayne still felt there was new cinematic territory to explore. And even though he was already the hottest star in Hollywood, he was right. With the 1968 Andrew V. McLaglen film *Hellfighters*, Duke stepped into the boots of a different kind of hero by playing a man who makes his living facing down hellacious blazes.

Having only worked together on the slapstick-fueled, quip-filled comedy *McLintock!* (1963) at that point, *Hellfighters* would task Wayne and McLaglen with shifting from amusing mud fights to hair-raising firefights. Being versatile professionals and natural collaborators, the change in tone was no problem for the pair. When it came to shaping the legend's character, Duke and the director took inspiration from real-life oil rig firefighter Red Adair to give the drama even more gravitas.

John Wayne's Chance Buckman is a man who must contend with not only the physical dangers of his career, but the toll it takes on his personal life. After being sidelined by an accident on the job, Buckman is engulfed with feelings of longing for his ex-wife Madelyn (Vera Miles) and concern for his estranged daughter Tish (Katharine Ross). On top of that, he must also wrestle with the stress of his new son-in-law, fellow firefighter Greg (Jim Hutton), facing the dangers he knows all too well. In the end, though, Buckman manages to extinguish his troubles as he returns to the job in heroic fashion and reunites with his loved ones.

Hellfighters received plenty of praise, with critics particularly enjoying its believable heroism. "The picture gives the last of the rugged individualists a chance to once again put his Mount Rushmore-like mug on the wide screen and sell his own marketable brand of virtuous vim and vigor," wrote *Newsweek*. *The Los Angeles Times* called the film "the quintessential John Wayne movie," adding, "With plenty of heroics, a couple of brawls and some dignified romancing, it's tailor-made to the Duke."

1. E.O. "Coots" Matthews, Paul "Red" Adair, John Wayne and Asger "Boots" Hansen on the set of *Hellfighters* (1968). 2. A custom mug commemorating the film. 3. John Wayne and Jim Hutton in a scene.

> *"A fellow as ugly as you are probably couldn't get to first base without a fire."*
>
> **—JOHN WAYNE AS CHANCE BUCKMAN**
>
> ★ ★ ★

True Grit

RELEASE 1969
DIRECTOR HENRY HATHAWAY

BY 1969, JOHN WAYNE'S on-screen persona was the paradigm of decency. But for all the admirable morality he had been so convincingly displaying for decades, Duke had yet to receive formal recognition in the form of an Oscar. Come the end of the decade, though, all that would change when the actor took the image of John Wayne and flipped the script.

When the rights to adapt Charles Portis's 1968 novel *True Grit* were up for purchase, several producers threw their hats in the ring, including Duke's son, Michael Wayne. After director Henry Hathaway called John Wayne to discuss the possibility of the actor taking part in the film if the bid went his and producer Hal Wallis's way, Duke's son gave him Portis's novel to familiarize himself with the story. Michael Wayne once recalled his father saying of the book, "I think it's great, and I hope you get it. But no matter who gets it, I'm gonna play that part." And play that part he did. "The character is a larger-than-life guy who refuses to fail against impossible odds," writes Scott Eyman in *John Wayne: The Life and Legend*. "And it's always nice for an actor to star in an adaptation of a book that was a large commercial success." Hathaway and Wallis would indeed get their hands on the rights to make *True Grit*, and Duke grabbed the reins of the role of Rooster Cogburn, put them in his teeth and got to work on turning in the finest performance of his career.

While Hathaway excelled at presenting a coherent plot with stunning cinematography, the director didn't give much guidance to his actors—especially John Wayne, a star he'd been working with on and off for decades. At first, Duke portrayed Rooster as broad as a barn side, but later dialed back the performance and found the tragedy of the marshal to balance out the humor. As Eyman says, "Playing loneliness was in John Wayne's wheelhouse, from

his characters in *She Wore a Yellow Ribbon* to *Sands of Iwo Jima*, but Rooster was unusual in that he expressed that loneliness openly," says Eyman. "That scene where Rooster describes how his wife and son don't like him very much.... That scene elevates John Wayne's performance into one worthy of the Academy Award."

And while Duke did finally fill his hand with a long-awaited Best

1. Henry Hathaway, Duke and Glen Campbell shoot *True Grit* (1969). **2.** Kim Darby, John Wayne and Glen Campbell on set. **3.** An eyepatch worn by Duke in the film **4.** Duke in a scene. **5.** John Wayne as Rooster Cogburn. **6.** A promotional banner for the film.

> *"Fill your hand,*
> *you son of a bitch!"*

—JOHN WAYNE AS ROOSTER COGBURN

★ ★ ★

A PARAMOUNT PICTURE

JOHN WAYNE

TRUE GRIT

TECHNICOLOR®

Actor Oscar in 1970, the Academy likely loved more than just the dramatic moments the legend showcased in the role. Rooster is bitter, foul-mouthed and stubborn—qualities that make him the right man for the job when the young Mattie Ross (Kim Darby) needs help finding her father's murderer, Tom Chaney (Jeff Corey). After Mattie is kidnapped and Texas Ranger LaBoeuf (Glen Campbell) is left for dead, Rooster comes to the rescue, killing Chaney and saving Mattie from a snake pit with the brazen courage of a man who's seen it all (through one eye). As they part ways at the end of the film, Rooster rides off in fitting fashion, telling Mattie to "come see a fat old man some time" before effortlessly leaping a fence on his horse.

Reflecting on the character's final moments in the film, Duke told Roger Ebert in a June 1969 interview, "I guess that scene in *True Grit* is about the best scene I ever did." The following year, the Academy would agree. After wiping a grateful tear from his eye as he stood on stage holding Oscar gold at the 42nd Academy Awards, the legend joked, "If I'd have known that, I'd have put that patch on 35 years earlier."

7. John Wayne in *True Grit*.
8. From left, standing: Glen Campbell, Duke, Jeremy Slate and Dennis Hopper in the film.
9. John Wayne accepts the 1970 Academy Award for Best Actor.

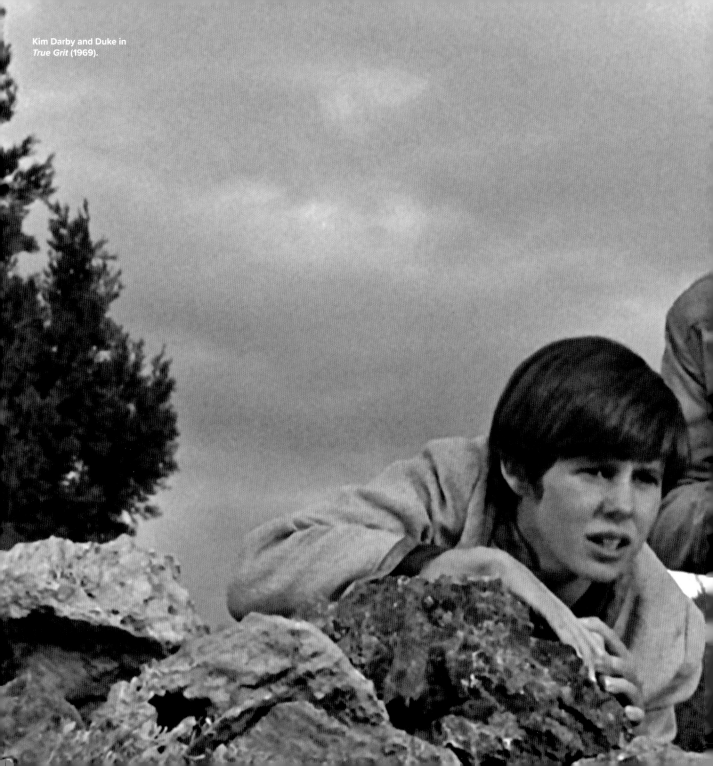

Kim Darby and Duke in
True Grit (1969).

During production, Duke's co-stars Roman Gabriel and Merlin Olsen were active members of the Los Angeles Rams football team.

The Undefeated

RELEASE 1969
DIRECTOR ANDREW V. MCLAGLEN

THIS POST-CIVIL WAR picture from *McLintock!* (1963) director Andrew V. McLaglen sees John Wayne as Union Colonel John Henry Thomas, a gruff Northerner forced to team up with a man he would've considered a foe in the recent past. After an ambush by Mexican bandits causes them to become unlikely temporary allies, Col. Thomas and his former adversary Confederate Col. James Langdon (Rock Hudson) soon find themselves in another situation that can only be resolved if they're able to unite as countrymen. Langdon and his crew are captured in Durango, and Thomas is told by the enemy troops that the Confederate crew will be killed unless the Union Colonel hands over his herd of horses. Recognizing who the true enemy is, Col. Thomas gives up the herd, saving the lives of the Southerners.

John Wayne
on the set of
Chisum (1970).

RIDING INTO THE SUNSET

Not one to go out with a whimper, John Wayne made sure his final years in film contained some of the finest work of his career.

Andrew V. McLaglen directed 96 episodes of *Gunsmoke*, which was first introduced to TV viewers by John Wayne on September 10, 1955.

Chisum

RELEASE 1970
DIRECTOR ANDREW V. MCLAGLEN

THE 1970S KICKED off with John Wayne delivering the goods in classic fashion as John Chisum, a cattle baron ready to do whatever it takes to defend the place he calls home. When the nefarious Lawrence Murphy (Forrest Tucker) begins to overtake many of the local businesses in Lincoln County, Chisum, one of the town's founders, is rightfully concerned. Ready to prevent his home from falling too far into the wrong hands, Chisum forms an alliance with Billy "The Kid" Bonney (Geoffrey Deuel), Henry Tunstall (Patric Knowles), James Pepper (Ben Johnson) and Pat Garett (Glenn Corbett). An all-out land war ensues, but Chisum knows he'll get his hands on the head honcho himself soon enough, telling Pepper, "No matter where people go, sooner or later there's the law."

The conflict culminates in a climax that sees Chisum bringing the fight to Murphy in an all-out barn burner at the bank. After the two men brawl onto the second floor of the business, a fire on the balcony sends both foes crashing to the ground below. Chisum makes it to his feet, and as he dusts himself off, he sees that Murphy has been impaled on a bull horn that had been lying on the ground.

Pleased to see Duke do what he does best, *The New York Daily News* called *Chisum*, "a mighty fine Western, made to order for the biggest Western star of them all."

Glenn Corbett, John Wayne and Ben Johnson in *Chisum* **(1970).**

John Wayne in *Rio Lobo* (1970). Inset: Duke on the set of the film.

Rio Lobo

RELEASE 1970
DIRECTOR HOWARD HAWKS

IN WHAT WOULD be their final film together, the proven power duo of John Wayne and Howard Hawks made sure to pull out all the stops for a wild cinematic ride they could proudly hang their hats on. Following the Civil War, Duke's former Union officer Cord McNally is hellbent on finding Ketcham (Victor French), whose treason during the conflict got many of McNally's men killed. After McNally rides into Rio Lobo, he learns the settlement has been taken over by Ketcham and his crew. With the opportunity to deliver the comeuppance practically presented to him on a silver platter, the former Union officer prepares his plan. When McNally finally finds Ketcham cornered in a house, he wastes no time avenging his fallen men with his fists. As he proceeds to make the man pay for his treasonous past, McNally tells his foe, "I've waited a long time for this."

Even after decades of seeing him deliver overdue justice, critics still delighted in seeing Duke take down the bad guys. "Wayne seems as natural and right in his role as a well-worn saddle," *Time* wrote in its review, continuing, "Duke knows by instinct what audiences will accept without question: whatever he may be called in the script, he is always unmistakably John Wayne. And who would have it any other way?"

John Wayne, Patrick
Wayne and Maureen
O'Hara in *Big Jake* (1971).

Big Jake

RELEASE 1971
DIRECTOR GEORGE SHERMAN

DESPITE IT BEING 1971, the same year Dirty Harry would draw a line in the sand for all future films starring hard-nosed heroes, John Wayne proved he was still as tough as they come in *Big Jake*. Known for his tough talk and tougher actions, Duke's Jacob McCandles has been disconnected from his wife Martha (Maureen O'Hara) and sons James (Patrick Wayne) and Jeff (Bobby Vinton) since deserting the family ranch 10 years prior. But when the heinous John Fain (Richard Boone) and his group of murderous outlaws storm the family's estate, murder the ranch hands and kidnap Little Jake McCandles—played by John Wayne's youngest son Ethan—Martha knows the boy's estranged grandfather is the only man fit for the task of bringing him home safely. Though the Texas Rangers and the Army offer to lead the mission, Martha knows the task will require an "extremely harsh and unpleasant kind of person to see it through" and sends a letter to her notorious husband asking for his help.

Without a moment of hesitation, McCandles gets on the next available train and heads home to track down his grandson and deliver hard-hitting justice along the way. Even when outmatched and outnumbered, he handles business with the fast fists and quick wit of a much younger man. "Oh, you've got me scared!" McCandles mockingly tells a foe in one scene, and when he finally arrives at Fain's hideout to rescue Little Jake, the gunslinging grandfather warns the villain, "Anything goes wrong, anything at all— your fault, my fault, nobody's fault, it don't matter…I'm gonna blow your head off." But John Wayne's virility in the role is perhaps best summed up early in the film when McCandles intervenes to prevent an unwarranted hanging: After one of the outlaws says he thought McCandles was dead, the fearsome old-timer replies, "Not hardly."

Clockwise from top left: Duke, Ethan Wayne, Maureen O'Hara, Christopher Mitchum, Bobby Vinton and Patrick Wayne on the set of *Big Jake* (1971).

> ## "You're short on ears and long on mouth!"
>
> **—JOHN WAYNE AS JACOB MCCANDLES**

★ ★ ★

John Wayne and the young ranch hands in *The Cowboys* (1972).

The Cowboys

RELEASE 1972
DIRECTOR MARK RYDELL

EQUAL PARTS HEARTWARMING and heartbreaking, *The Cowboys* (1972) combined all of John Wayne's greatest cinematic strengths to deliver an unforgettable late entry in the legend's career. As Wil Andersen, an aging rancher in dire need of help on his cattle drive after his ranch hands abandon him to go searching for gold, Duke is immediately presented with a vulnerability not often seen. When a local man recommends Andersen train some schoolboys to work for him, the rancher goes to the school to scope out some of the prospects. Though he remains wary of the idea of hiring inexperienced greenhorns, he decides to make the most of the opportunity when several of the boys eagerly show up for duty at his ranch the next day.

Not only does Andersen teach the boys how to do the grueling work required on his cattle drive, he also imparts the value of such work upon them. And fortunately for all involved, the boys prove to be fast learners who go from tenderfoots to fine cowhands. But just as the relationship between the weathered rancher and his hired help is truly beginning to evolve, Andersen is shot by the outlaw Long Hair (Bruce Dern), who steals the herd. The boys find Wil dying from his wounds the next morning, but the de facto father figure makes sure to tell them what they mean to him before he goes: "I'm proud of ya...all of ya. Every man wants his children to be better than he was. You are."

In its review of the film, *The New York Times* commended the legend for tapping into his softer side, writing, "Wayne is, of course, marvelously indestructible and he has become an almost perfect father figure." And the impression Duke made with *The Cowboys* has indeed proven to be "indestructible." One of the schoolboys from the film, Norman Howell, has since gone on to become a prolific stunt coordinator. In an interview with *LA 411*, Howell discussed helping *Brooklyn Nine-Nine*'s Stephanie Beatriz with a challenging fight scene using something he learned from the legend: "I taught her the punch John Wayne taught me on my first movie, *The Cowboys*."

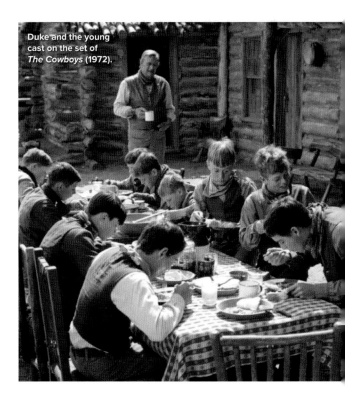

Duke and the young cast on the set of *The Cowboys* (1972).

"Slap some bacon on a biscuit and let's go! We're burnin' daylight!"

—JOHN WAYNE AS WIL ANDERSEN

★ ★ ★

John Wayne, Clay O'Brien, Alfred Barker Jr., A Martinez (on horse), Stephen R. Hudis, Nicolas Beauvy (kneeling), Sean Kelly, Mike Pyeatt (on horse), Roscoe Lee Browne, Steve Benedict, Norman Howell (on horse), Robert Carradine (standing) and Sam O'Brien on the set of *The Cowboys* (1972).

Cancel My Reservation

RELEASE 1972
DIRECTOR PAUL BOGART

IN SOMEWHAT OF a full-circle moment, this 1972 film sees John Wayne returning to his roots in a brief, uncredited role—the difference being that this time, he was a major star who could simply play himself. Duke's pal Bob Hope stars in this comedic mystery as Dan Bartlett, a struggling talk show host who takes a vacation only to find himself the main suspect of a series of murders. After being imprisoned, Barlett asks himself, "Where's John Wayne when you need him?" which causes Duke to magically appear in the cell only to tell Bartlett he can't help him.

The Train Robbers

RELEASE 1973
DIRECTOR BURT KENNEDY

THIS GOOD OLD-FASHIONED Western sees John Wayne teaming up with eventual Hollywood legend Ann-Margret in a story centered on the prospect of gold in a Texas railroad town. Hoping for a fresh start, Ann-Margret's widow, Mrs. Lowe, hires Duke's Union veteran Lane to track down the gold her late husband stole. Praising the icon's ability to continue elevating the genre he'd already perfected, *Variety* called the film, "an above-average John Wayne actioner... with suspense, comedy and humanism not usually found in the formula."

Ben Johnson, Christopher George, Rod Taylor, Ann-Margret and Duke in *The Train Robbers* (1973).

Cahill U.S. Marshal

RELEASE 1973
DIRECTOR ANDREW V. MCLAGLEN

IN THIS FINAL entry from frequent collaborators John Wayne and Andrew V. McLaglen, Duke's titular lawman finds himself in an extreme example of being caught between a rock and a hard place. After returning home from duty one day, widower J.D. Cahill learns that the local bank has been robbed. To make matters worse, it soon becomes clear his own sons Danny (Gary Grimes) and Billy (Clay O'Brien), who have joined a gang in his absence, are the perpetrators. It's a lose-lose situation for the fearsome marshal, who can either turn in his boys or violate the very code he lives by.

Critics were impressed with John Wayne's ability to hold tight to his unshakable persona while simultaneously playing a man faced with a terrible ultimatum. *The New York Daily News* wrote, "Wayne gives his usual pro performance acting himself," adding, "He is smooth and effortless." *Variety*, meanwhile, praised Duke's believability in the role, writing, "Wayne carries out characterization realistically and gets firm support right down the line."

McQ

RELEASE 1974
DIRECTOR JOHN STURGES

WHILE SEVERAL DIFFERENT points of John Wayne's career did see him portraying various sheriffs sporting 10-gallon hats and star-shaped badges, it wasn't until 1974 that the legend starred as a more modern lawman in a gritty police drama. The genre had become quite popular during the decade thanks to television series such as *Kojak* and *Police Story*, and Hollywood was aiming to bring that success to the big screen. When John Wayne stepped into the titular role in *McQ* (1974), the standard for tough-talking, no-nonsense cop characters was taken to a new level.

Beyond being an opportunity for the legend to freshen up his filmography late in the game, *McQ* also gave John Wayne the chance to work with director John Sturges for the first time. Like Duke, Sturges was mostly known for his mastery of the Western, with a decades-spanning career yielding classics including *Gunfight at the O.K. Corral* (1957) and *The Magnificent Seven* (1960). For *McQ*, however, the director and the icon would trade the sturdy steeds and dusty trails of the Old West for the fast cars and moody streets of Seattle.

The film sees John Wayne as Lieutenant Lon "McQ" McHugh, an Emerald City detective hellbent on catching the man who killed his partner and two other officers in a mysterious shooting spree. Suspecting a local drug lord to be the perpetrator, McQ goes rogue and violently interrogates the man, which leads to his removal from the case. Undeterred, the gruff detective manages to get himself hired as a private

"The hell I can't!"

—JOHN WAYNE AS LON McQ

★ ★ ★

investigator instead and continues to pursue justice. In the process of finding the man who murdered his partner, though, McQ uncovers corruption within his own police department. With his one-versus-all mentality reinforced even further, the veteran lawman goes full tilt in a series of heart-stopping shootouts and high-speed car chases across the city of Seattle.

Eager to promote his debut venture into the neo-noir '70s cop genre, Duke took unique opportunities to get the word out ahead of the film's release. On January 15, 1974, he accepted a satirical award from *The Harvard Lampoon* and playfully debated the Ivy Leaguers, earning numerous national headlines and further interest in *McQ*. That same month, the legend journeyed to London to promote the police drama on a Glen Campbell television special.

With plenty of eyes on his portrayal of the lone wolf cop, Duke didn't disappoint. "The many fans of John Wayne will be happy to know he's as effective in a crime-ridden police force as he has been in the saddle," *The New York Post* wrote in its review, adding, "John Wayne can do anything he sets his face to, and pretty well, at that."

1. John Wayne takes aim as Lt. Lon "McQ" McHugh in *McQ* (1974). **2.** Duke's annotated script for the film. **3.** A *McQ* windbreaker jacket worn by the cast and crew. **4.** John Wayne in a scene from the film. **5.** A promotional poster for the film.

Brannigan

RELEASE 1975
DIRECTOR DOUGLAS HICKOX

N 1975, WHAT would ultimately be the penultimate year of his career, John Wayne had nothing left to prove. But like the characters he played over the course of nearly half a century on the silver screen, Duke was always willing to be thrown into deep waters to remind himself that he still knew how to swim. So just before his career came to a close, the icon bravely traveled across the pond to star in the thrilling crime film *Brannigan* (1975).

In many ways, *Brannigan* was evidence of John Wayne's willingness to embrace the changing of the guard in Hollywood. In addition to being his second time leaning into the loner cop trend of the 1970s, the film marked the first occasion in which the legend worked with English director Douglas Hickox, who, at the time, was still an up-and-coming filmmaker looking to make a splash with a big name like John Wayne. Brannigan also gave Duke the chance to work with Richard Attenborough, a fellow prolific actor and director who would later win two Oscars for *Gandhi* (1982) and enjoy a renaissance in the 1990s with his roles in the classics *Jurassic Park* (1993) and *Miracle on 34th Street* (1994).

John Wayne wastes no time making his incomparable presence felt in the film as his grizzled Chicago cop Lieutenant Jim Brannigan is sent to London to take an American mobster into custody. Upon his arrival, Brannigan is confronted by crooks and hitmen who try to interfere with his business, but the bad guys quickly learn that age is nothing but a number in the case of this aging lawman. The lieutenant follows through on his quippy threats, allowing his foes only a moment to doubt his physical capabilities before finding themselves on the losing side of pub brawls and wild shootouts. In one standout scene, a hitman makes the mistake of attempting to take Brannigan out in a drive-by shooting. Firing a few shots through the windshield, Brannigan sends the hired killer's car careening off a London pier, proving Duke could be just as formidable in the modern

1. John Wayne on the set of *Brannigan* (1975). **2.** A porcelain Royal Doulton English bulldog given to Duke by the cast and crew. **3.** A promotional British quad for the film. **4.** Brian Glover and Duke in a scene.

era as he always was in the Wild West.

In its review of the film, *The New York Post* praised Duke for his performance "in the hard-guy role he has always filled with fist, gun and granite law," adding, "John Wayne is a tested, guaranteed product, and so is this picture."

Rooster Cogburn

RELEASE 1975
DIRECTOR STUART MILLAR

FIVE YEARS AFTER the role of the cantankerous marshal in *True Grit* (1969) won him his lone Academy Award, John Wayne traveled to Oregon to begin shooting essentially the only true sequel he ever made, 1975's *Rooster Cogburn*. While director Stuart Millar would be at the helm this time rather than Henry Hathaway, Duke would still work with a familiar face in producer Hal Wallis, Hathaway's right-hand man who helped shepherd *True Grit* to greatness. As for his co-star this time around, John Wayne would be sharing the screen with one of the few cinematic legends he'd never worked with before: Katharine Hepburn.

Mirroring the reality of Duke and Hepburn teaming up for the first time, the film sees Rooster Cogburn joining up with an unlikely ally in Hepburn's Eulah Goodnight, a missionary hoping to bring her father's murderer to justice. Much like how Rooster discovers Eulah is more than capable of holding her own in the film—which sees the missionary fearlessly ambushing outlaws on horseback—John Wayne quickly developed a fondness for Hepburn's similar grit behind the scenes. When shooting began, the actress was only months removed from having hip surgery—a display of toughness that likely reminded Duke of shooting *The Sons of Katie Elder* (1965) fresh out of life-saving lung surgery 10 years prior.

The film had two working titles: *Rooster Cogburn and the Lady* and *Rooster Cogburn: A Man of True Grit.*

John Wayne and Katharine Hepburn in *Rooster Cogburn* (1975).

Strother Martin,
Katharine Hepburn and
John Wayne in *Rooster
Cogburn* (1975).

The Shootist

RELEASE 1976
DIRECTOR DON SIEGEL

THE SHOOTIST (1976) was never meant to be John Wayne's final film, but Duke couldn't have asked for a better way to finish his incredible career on the big screen. Director Don Siegel's meditative Western gave the aging icon the chance to star in a story about regret, redemption and hope for the future. And like the real Duke, the film's legendary gunslinger J.B. Books is a man who operates with supreme confidence, never wavering from his code no matter the circumstances.

While the film fires on all cylinders as a finished product, Duke and the director encountered a few bumps on the road to success. Although Siegel's work won him two Oscars relatively early in his career (for the 1945 short films *Hitler Lives* and *Star in the Night*) and he had already helmed a number of successful films by the time of *The Shootist* (including 1971's *Dirty Harry*), the filmmaker had never before dealt with a star possessing both the experience and formidable will of John Wayne. Duke, who had spent decades working with John Ford and directed *The Alamo* (1960) and *The Green Berets* (1968) himself, would sometimes butt heads with Siegel over how to frame a particular shot. The give and take between director and star may have led to a few tense moments on set, but both men were professionals and kept their tempers in check. In fact, Duke's co-stars had nothing but praise for the legend's attitude and demeanor during filming, despite suffering a variety of health ailments. "He was amazing all through that shoot," co-star Lauren Bacall, who played Bond Rogers, said in an interview with Larry King in 2005. "He never complained...and he was terrific."

Bacall, who had previously starred alongside John Wayne in 1955's *Blood Alley*, was one of several old friends who worked on what was to be the star's last film. Other old acquaintances included Richard Boone and, most famously, Jimmy Stewart, who had retired from acting. The familiar faces were just another example of how *The Shootist* melded its plot and themes with John Wayne's own life, as the film casts Duke as gunfighter J.B. Books, an old man confronting his legacy in his final days. After receiving a diagnosis of terminal cancer from old friend Doc Hostetler (Stewart), Books spends his time in Carson City, Nevada, at a boarding house, usually in the company of either the landlady Bond Rogers (Bacall) or her teenage son Gillom, played by Ron Howard.

In contrast to the sweeping epics he made with John Ford or the tense oaters he starred in for Howard Hawks, *The Shootist* is a film of quiet decisions. How does Books deal with the hordes of hangers-on, from ex-wives to newspapermen to undertakers, who want to cash in on his demise and reputation? Will the impressionable Gillom follow the example of Books's younger days and raise hell, or will he eschew a life of violence? Can Books find his way to a "good death," and what does that even mean for the gunman? Books eventually resolves the last question by inviting three old foes to a saloon so all parties involved can have the chance to finally settle their lingering scores. But though Books bests the trio in the ensuing firefight, he's blasted from behind by the shotgun-wielding bartender, causing the onlooking Gillom to run in and mourn his hero as he takes his final breath.

As a young actor whose career was just beginning to truly take off at the time, Ron Howard was particularly impressed with Duke's work in the Western. "I always admired him as a movie star, but I thought of him as a total naturalist," Howard told Brian Williams at the Tribeca Film Festival in 2014. "[H]e's working on this scene and he's like, 'Let me try this again.' And he put the little hitch in, and he'd

1. John Wayne and Charles G. Martin (bartender) in *The Shootist* (1976). **2.** A shirt, vest and tie worn by Duke in the film. **3.** John Wayne's annotated script. **4.** Duke and James Stewart between takes.

find the Wayne rhythm and you'd realize that it changed the performance each and every time."

Beyond the top-notch acting skills Duke displayed, critics were struck by the close-to-home poignancy of John Wayne portraying a legendary man dying of cancer in what would be the star's final role. *Newsweek* praised the star's "proud, quietly anguished performance," adding that it "has a richness that seems born of self-knowledge," while *The New York Daily News* wrote: "This is unmistakably Wayne's valedictory performance. Only a great actor could have given this skillfully delineated performance." If John Wayne's career had to end, there could be no better note to end on than that of the impeccably strong-willed J.B. Books.

---

5. A promotional British quad for *The Shootist*.
6. Lauren Bacall and Duke between takes on set.
7. John Wayne in a scene from the film.

The film shot on location in Carson City, Nevada and at Warner Bros. Studios, Burbank.

AFTERWORD

BY LEONARD MALTIN, FILM HISTORIAN

JOHN WAYNE WAS larger than life. That's one of the qualities we used to admire in a movie star. It didn't hurt that the ex-football player stood 6 feet 4 inches tall, towering over his leading ladies and most of his co-stars (a memorable exception came when he introduced his protégé, James Arness, on the debut episode of *Gunsmoke*—the man who would become famous as Marshal Dillon was 3 inches taller than Duke).

He never thought of himself as a great actor. Even moviegoers who liked him said "he always played himself," which of course isn't true, any more than it was true of other stars who crafted public personas. The drawling, lovable Jimmy Stewart was a creation that took over where the great actor left off, and the same could be said of John Wayne. After the glory years of *Red River*, *She Wore a Yellow Ribbon*, *The Quiet Man* and *The Searchers*—four films that demonstrated beyond question Duke's range as an actor—he settled into a series of comfortable star vehicles that played to his strengths and gave the audience what they wanted to see.

Making those movies kept John Wayne in the chips and at the top of the box-office polls far longer than he could have anticipated. But let's not forget that he paid his dues for nine hard years before getting his true shot at stardom. Watch John Ford's *Stagecoach* again and you'll see how that decade of experience paid off. There is no sign of a rookie stepping up to bat

John Wayne in *The Searchers* (1956).

for the first time. He holds his own with some of the most experienced actors in Hollywood, not to mention leading lady Claire Trevor. He's a "natural," comfortable in his boots and commanding the attention of that camera lens from his first moment on screen.

Imagine how frustrating it must have been to play characters as diverse as Captain Nathan Brittles and Ethan Edwards and still be taken for granted by critics and even fans. That's where posterity comes into play. We aren't bound by old-fashioned notions of what constitutes an exceptional performance. We know it when we see it. John Wayne was a great star and when it mattered most, a great actor as well.

INDEX

PHOTOGRAPHY CREDITS

COVER: WAYNE FELLOWS PRODUCTIONS/RONALD GRANT ARCHIVE/ALAMY. DIGITAL COLORIZATION BY LORNA CLARK
BACK COVER: PICTURELUX/THE HOLLYWOOD ARCHIVE/ALAMY

2 Everett Collection; 6 Everett Collection; 8 20th Century Fox/Everett Collection; 10 Everett Collection/Alamy; 11 Everett Collection; 12 20th Century Fox/Everett Collection; 13 20th Century Fox/Everett Collection; 14 SilverScreen/Alamy; 15 JJs/Alamy; 18 20th Century Fox/Everett Collection; 19 Fox/Photofest; 20 20th Century Fox/Everett Collection; 22 PictureLux/The Hollywood Archive/Alamy; 25 PictureLux/The Hollywood Archive/Alamy; 26 Collection Christophel/Alamy; 26 TCD/Prod.DB/Alamy; 27 Ronald Grant Archive/Alamy; 28 Bettmann/Getty Images; 29 20th Century Fox/Everett Collection; 29 Collection Christophel/Alamy; 30 Everett Collection/Alamy; 32 Everett Collection; 33 Everett Collection; 35 Everett Collection; 36 Monogram/Kobal/Shutterstock; 42 Everett Collection; 44 Everett Collection; 49 CineClassico/Alamy; 51 Everett Collection; 52 Republic Pictures/Photofest; 55 Pictorial Press Ltd/Alamy; 57 Photo 12/Alamy; 61 Everett Collection; 62 Everett Collection; 64 Everett Collection; 67 TCD/Prod.DB/Alamy; 68 Ned Scott/United Artists/Kobal/Shutterstock; 68 Everett Collection/Alamy; 69 UA/Photofest; 70 Phoenix/Alamy; 72 Ned Scott/United Artists/Kobal/Shutterstock; 76 Jerry Tavin/Everett Collection; 77 Everett Collection; 81 Everett Collection; 84 Michael Ochs Archives/Getty Images; 90 AF Archive/Alamy; 91 Everett Collection; 91 Album/Alamy; 92 Masheter Movie Archive/Alamy; 93 Photo 12/Alamy; 97 Republic Pictures/Photofest; 98 Universal Pictures/Photofest; 99 Everett Collection; 100 Everett Collection; 104 Everett Collection; 107 Courtesy U.S. Navy Seabee Museum; 108 Everett Collection; 109 TCD/Prod.DB/Alamy; 116 Everett Collection; 117 TCD/Prod.DB/Alamy; 123 Everett Collection; 125 Everett Collection; 126 Everett Collection; 128 AF Archive/Alamy; 130 Photo 12/Alamy; 131 TCD/Prod.DB/Alamy; 131 Allstar Picture Library Ltd/Alamy; 132 Everett Collection; 134 Collection Christophel/Alamy; 135 TCD/Prod.DB/Alamy; 136 Everett Collection; 137 Everett Collection; 138 Pictorial Press Ltd/Alamy; 141 Pictorial Press Ltd/Alamy; 142 Ronald Grant Archive/Alamy; 143 Everett Collection; 144 ScreenProd/Photononstop/Alamy; 145 Collection Christophel/Alamy; 150 Photo 12/Alamy; 152 AA Film Archive/Alamy; 155 Album/Alamy; 156 TCD/Prod.DB/Alamy; 160 Everett Collection; 161 Everett Collection; 162 Collection Christophel/Alamy; 163 Collection Christophel/Alamy; 163 Everett Collection; 164 Everett Collection; 165 Photo 12/Alamy; 166 TCD/Prod.DB/Alamy; 167 Everett Collection; 168 TCD/Prod.DB/Alamy; 170 TCD/Prod.DB/Alamy; 171 Everett Collection; 171 Moviestore Collection Ltd/Alamy; 172 Masheter Movie Archive/Alamy; 172 ScreenProd/Photononstop/Alamy; 173 TCD/Prod.DB/Alamy; 174 TCD/Prod.DB/Alamy; 176 Porges/Ullstein Bild via Getty Images; 179 Everett Collection; 180 Everett Collection; 182 John Springer Collection/Corbis via Getty Images; 185 ScreenProd/Photononstop/Alamy; 187 Warner Bros Pictures/Sunset Boulevard/Corbis via Getty Images; 188 Everett Collection; 188 Photo 12/Alamy; 189 AF Archive/Alamy; 189 Everett Collection; 190 Everett Collection/Alamy; 191 AF Archive/Alamy; 191 Pictorial Press Ltd/Alamy; 192 TCD/Prod.DB/Alamy; 193 Everett Collection; 198 ScreenProd/Photononstop/Alamy; 199 Bettmann/Getty Images; 199 UA/Photofest; 200 United Artists/Sunset Boulevard/Corbis via Getty Images; 201 Everett Collection; 201 Zuma Press/Alamy; 202 AF Archive/Alamy; 206 TCD/Prod.DB/Alamy; 207 Collection Christophel/Alamy; 207 Twentieth Century Fox Film Corporation/Diltz/Bridgeman Images; 210 Shutterstock; 213 Ronald Grant Archive/Alamy; 215 Allstar Picture Library Ltd/Alamy; 216 Paramount Pictures/Ronald Grant Archive/Mary Evans/Alamy; 219 Everett Collection; 220 Susan Wood/Getty Images; 221 Moviestore Collection Ltd/Alamy; 222 Everett Collection (2); 223 Susan Wood/Getty Images; 224 AF Archive/Alamy; 226 Twentieth Century Fox/Photofest; 227 Everett Collection; 228 TCD/Prod.DB/Alamy; 229 Album/Alamy; 230 Collection Christophel/Alamy; 231 AF Archive/Alamy; 232 TCD/Prod.DB/Alamy; 234 John Springer Collection/Corbis via Getty Images; 236 Album/Alamy; 237 Everett Collection; 238 Paramount Pictures/Sunset Boulevard/Corbis via Getty Images; 240 Everett Collection; 240 Collection Christophel/Alamy; 241 AF Archive/Alamy; 243 Silver Screen Collection/Getty Images; 243 Everett Collection; 244 Silver Screen Collection/Getty Images; 246 Allstar Picture Library Ltd/Alamy; 248 Entertainment Pictures/Alamy; 249 Photo 12/Alamy; 250 Sunset Boulevard/Corbis via Getty Images; 252 Universal/Kobal/Shutterstock; 255 TCD/Prod.DB/Alamy; 256 Photo 12/Alamy; 257 TCD/Prod.DB/Alamy; 258 Collection Christophel/Alamy; 259 Warner Brothers/Getty Images; 259 Collection Christophel/Alamy; 261 MARKA/Alamy; 263 Collection Christophel/Alamy; 264 Paramount/Kobal/Shutterstock; 267 Everett Collection; 267 Bettmann/Getty Images; 268 Collection Christophel/Alamy; 272 Michael Ochs Archives/Getty Images; 275 Everett Collection; 276 Malabar/Cinema Center/Kobal/Shutterstock; 277 Everett Collection/Alamy; 278 Paramount/Everett Collection; 280 Everett Collection; 281 Photo 12/Alamy; 282 Collection Christophel/Alamy; 284 ScreenProd/Photononstop/Alamy; 286 Photo 12/Alamy; 287 Pictorial Press Ltd/Alamy; 288 Terry Fincher Photo Int/Alamy; 289 Everett Collection; 290 Abaca Press/Alamy; 291 Everett Collection; 292 Photo 12/Alamy; 296 Silver Screen Collection/Getty Images; 299 AF Archive/Alamy; Courtesy Heritage Auctions: 4, 79, 85, 89 (2), 90, 106, 107 (2), 109, 117, 130 (2), 134, 140, 143, 149 (3), 155 (2), 161, 162, 171, 179 (2), 180, 189 (2), 198, 199, 200, 207 (2), 212, 214 (2), 221 (2), 232, 240, 256 (2), 259, 260, 264, 265, 287 (3), 289 (2), 294 (2), 296

Media Lab Books
For inquiries, call 646-449-8614

Copyright 2022 Topix Media Lab

Published by Topix Media Lab
14 Wall Street, Suite 3C
New York, NY 10005

Printed in Korea

ISBN-13: 978-1-948174-83-1
ISBN-10: 1-948174-83-9